HEARST MARINE BOOKS
CANOEING BASICS

HEARST MARINE BOOKS
CANOEING BASICS

Melinda Allan

Illustrations by Ron Carboni

HEARST MARINE BOOKS

New York

Library of Congress Cataloging-in-Publication Data

Allan, Melinda.
  Hearst Marine books canoeing basics / Melinda Allan. – 1st ed.
    p.   cm.
  Includes index.
  ISBN 0-688-12476-3
  1. Canoes and canoeing.   I. Title.
GV783.A44   1994
797.1'22—dc20   93-37869
                                                                CIP

Printed in the United States of America

First Edition

1 2 3 4 5 6 7 8 9 10

BOOK DESIGN BY GIORGETTA BELL McREE

ACKNOWLEDGMENTS

Thanks to Mel Jackson, Chris Culver and his canoeing class, plus Tom Mooney and the staff of River Runner Supply.

And especially to Al, who took me on my first canoe trip, down a cold river in winter ("You did want to go through the expert route, didn't you?"), and patiently endured photo sessions as well as artistic temperament flare-ups.

CONTENTS

CHAPTER 1

CANOES: BACK TO BASICS

Close your eyes and imagine yourself in the middle of a placid lake. Listen to waves lapping against your boat, the cry of a loon shoreside. No other sound intrudes. Now savor fresh pure air. Pine trees. Spring blossoms. Far from stress and smog, your only concern is matching the rhythm of your partner's paddle stroke. You might be in the barrens of the Far North, or on a pond a few miles' drive from home—the sensation remains the same. You are free.

Too peaceful? Then envision a wild ride down a whitewater stream, heart thumping, shouting directions to your partner, or just shouting to release your exhilaration. Feel the spray of haystacks breaking over the bow of your canoe. Yes, the same canoe that just took you across the wilderness lake. A design almost identical to those used by Native Americans and early explorers, the do-everything vessel for adventurers of all callings. Whether your quest is peaceful escape or thundering rapids, remote backcountry or the local reservoir, taking the kids camping or floating the Yukon solo for three months, paddling solo for an afternoon or with a group of dozens for a weekend—the adaptable, dependable canoe is your vehicle.

With the broad array of modern boats, inflatables, and exotic craft to choose from, why do canoes continue to be the world's most popular boats? The reasons are as varied as the people who become avid canoeists. Probably the canoe's strongest appeal is affordability—good canoes can be purchased new for several hundred dollars. Quality used canoes are easy to locate as well. And buying a canoe is a good investment, as most retain 50 percent or more of their original value. Most canoes on the market are well made, dependable, solid craft, so you get

good value for your money, without worrying about getting a lemon.

If you're not ready to buy, or don't have room for a canoe, rentals are widely available, at reasonable rates. Even entire camping/canoeing outfits can be rented, allowing first-time wilderness adventurers to sample the boating lifestyle. If you're uncertain of your outdoor expertise, you can hire guides along with the canoes and gear to show you how, keep you on the correct route, and even cook dinner for you and your family or group. Across the world, varied organizations provide canoe instruction: paddling clubs, college and university classes, Red Cross courses, Boy Scout merit badge programs, outdoor schools, river outfitters. These will give you a taste of what canoeing is like, with little investment other than your time and interest.

Canoeing is a great way for novice boaters to get their feet wet, because it's easy to learn. Just about everyone can wield a paddle well enough to move a canoe across flatwater. With a little instruction on techniques and some practice, beginners can tackle big lakes and moderate rivers. Paddling a canoe is not a mysterious lost art—it's a skill that can be readily absorbed and put to practical use, even by klutzes. The canoe is reasonably forgiving of mistakes, too. Don't be intimidated by lengthy lists of complicated canoe strokes—you can get by with less than half a dozen to start. The basic motions of forward and backward paddling can be mastered within minutes.

Getting a boat to the water's edge has never been simpler. Canoes are easy to transport, needing only the most basic of roof racks, with no hassles of backing a trailer down a boat ramp. Instead of waiting in line to launch your boat, just carry the canoe around all the confusion and you're ready to go. Also, storage and maintenance are a breeze, especially with today's space-age materials.

Families with younger children who can't hike or backpack find the canoe provides the perfect means to keep in touch with the outdoors. A standard seventeen-foot canoe easily transports an entire family into a wilderness setting. When the kids are older, they can advance to their own canoe. Also, by taking advantage of the option to float gear in addition to people, you can transport a good-sized load efficiently, without straining your muscles. Remember that the average person can paddle much more weight than he/she could ever carry in a backpack, and weight can actually add to the canoe's stability. With a canoe, you can pack along an ice chest to enjoy cold drinks or steak dinners, even deep in the wilderness. For load capacity of a lightweight boat, the canoe is unmatched.

Both men and women enjoy canoeing, together or separately. Because today's canoes are so lightweight, it's even easier for women to paddle solo, without having to rely on a partner to lift and carry the canoe. But even if you relish solitude, sharing the carrying and paddling chores with a compatible partner adds a new dimension to canoeing. Too independent? Then perhaps each partner could be in charge of a solo canoe, one of the fastest-growing dimensions of canoeing.

And just as size or sex is no barrier to handling a canoe, disabled individuals can also enjoy canoeing. Once a canoeist is seated, only moderate upper-body usage is required to send the canoe gliding along. Canoes offer one of the few non-motorized ways for the handicapped to sample real wilderness. About the only real barrier in canoeing is one's determination level—with assistance from a canoeing partner, even a severely handicapped person can be paddling or floating along. Some fiercely independent folks even use

Canoes go through narrow passages and other waters where bigger boats can't.

Paddling instruction is widely available, as well as inexpensive and fun.

a trailer with a winch so they can load and launch their canoe solo. You don't have to be permanently disabled to appreciate canoeing as a low-impact sport, either. People recovering from lower-body injuries can participate in canoeing while other favorite activities are on hold. Seniors, too, flock to canoeing as a moderate alternative to backpacking or biking.

Though the exercise is milder, canoeing still enhances health: paddling increases muscle tone without exhaustion or strain. Despite common perception, canoeing isn't necessarily bad for the knees. Kneeling—while recommended in heavy whitewater—isn't necessary or even practical during an all-day float. You can learn the special "relief positions" that accommodate sore knees or rigid lower bodies so that you can paddle confidently from the position that best suits your personal style.

Paddling is also relaxing, a soothing salve for the stress of modern life. On a big calm lake, there are no traffic jams or demanding bosses to cope with—just the gentle lap of waves against the side of the canoe. Plus, canoe ownership is refreshingly simple compared to the paperwork and bother of bigger boats. Nonmotorized canoes don't require yearly license fees or costly insurance, and there are none of the hassles, expenses, and environmental concerns connected with powerboats. Paddling is an efficient, quiet way to propel a boat just about anywhere you want to go. On the other hand, should you desire to add a motor, the versatile canoe can handle some horsepower. Also, unlike its bigger, cumbersome cousins, the canoe is at home in deep or shallow water—easily skimming over gravel bars or through reed-choked sloughs, to fish a secret bass hot spot or to watch, silent and unnoticed, the parade of wildlife drawn to the water's edge.

There's more to canoeing than just paddling around, too. Canoeing opens a new world of related activities, such as fishing, gold panning, nature study, and photography. You can often get very close to birds and animals while gliding along in a quiet canoe. Canoeing and camping are a natural combination, or you can even go inn-to-inn on your next float, overnighting in civilized luxury and paddling with a light load.

About the only limit to what a canoeist can accomplish is his or her own imagination. For the adventurous, canoes offer a vehicle into untracked wilderness, or through exhilarating whitewater. Canoes boast a long and rich history of exploration on this continent, and every civilization began with adventurers in small boats. Bold canoeists in Polynesia traversed the expansive Pacific in search of new islands. Modern canoeists may seek something as elusive as personal awareness or a sense of accomplishment, but the goal of exploring the great unknown remains the same. Whether you seek contentment, escape, risk, or family togetherness, the canoe is your craft.

CHAPTER 2

CHOOSING THE CORRECT CANOE FOR YOU

The first canoes were made of natural materials: dugout logs, tree bark, even reeds bundled together. Later, wood strips and canvas were viewed as ultramodern refinements. Today, good canoes are constructed from many synthetic materials, in addition to the traditional wood. Besides influencing appearance, cost, and weight, construction materials and methods help determine how a canoe handles on the water, and what care a canoe may need off the water. Because canoes have been around so long, their basic banana shape has been refined and improved, offering more choices in designs as well as materials. Take some time to look at canoe materials and shapes—how each change influences a canoe's handling characteristics.

At first glance, the array of canoe materials, designs, and shapes available can be confusing. Currently, there are over one hundred canoe manufacturers, with many offering ten or more models. Also tempting the first-time canoe buyer are "hybrids" such as inflatables. To narrow the field, define what you expect from your canoe. Despite manufacturers' claims, no one canoe can do everything. Every canoe design is a trade-off, with each design characteristic or hull material offering both advantages and disadvantages. Also keep in mind that some canoes perform adequately in varied environments—flatwater, rapids, or expeditions—while other models are more specialized. A boat built specifically for whitewater will never be an all-purpose canoe.

Consider hull design and material, durability, how the canoe is outfitted (seat placement, etc.), size (length, width, depth), weight, handling characteristics, cost, aesthetics (how the canoe looks), and load capacity. And think about which usage category appeals to you: expedition canoes for long trips with lots of carrying capacity, whitewater canoes that turn on a dime and resist rock damage, cruising and racing canoes built for speed, touring canoes and casual recreation canoes that try to please everyone.

CRITERIA FOR CHOOSING A CANOE

1. What canoe activities interest you most? Nervous novices will want a stable canoe, while adventurers prefer one that can handle heavy water. High performance is not necessary in a family canoe. But keep a broad outlook. You don't want to get an "all-purpose" canoe so unseaworthy that you're in trouble anytime wind comes up on the lake.

2. How many people will the canoe carry? And will it occasionally carry gear for camping? Make sure you get a canoe big enough to fit everyone and their belongings. An overloaded canoe is dangerous. If you envision month-long expeditions, carrying capacity is especially important. Will you want a tandem or solo canoe?

3. How heavy can the canoe be? Will you need to portage the canoe often? Can you lift that eighty-pound aluminum canoe easily, or should you pay more for a lighter weight? A canoe for solo paddlers or smaller-sized paddlers obviously must weigh less.

4. How durable is the canoe? A beginner will make mistakes, so a stronger canoe is desirable. And even experts like a canoe that lasts, for its resale value if nothing else. Sturdy canoes tend to be heavier, or more expensive, than less rugged models, but are worth the investment in weight and dollars over the long haul.

Most serious canoeists own more than one canoe. They began with an all-purpose, then took up running rivers, or racing, or their family grew up, so they added a specialized second canoe. Then there are beginners who find themselves fascinated by whitewater from the start, promptly purchasing the canoe of their dreams and working on skills.

The canoe market is reasonably competitive, yet not cutthroat. Expect to spend somewhere between $450 and $1,000 for a new, well-designed pleasure canoe, and more for special features or high-performance hulls, expensive hull materials like Kevlar, or super lightweight models. Generally, you get what you pay for—a cheap canoe usually means poor design, inferior materials, and diminished performance, unless you pick up a used canoe bargain. You may not enjoy canoeing if you buy a bad canoe, and you may never even know that the poor design of the canoe was to blame. Canoe sellers range from the local discount store to custom canoe builders. Usually a "name" canoe manufacturer means a better quality canoe, as manufacturers of serious canoes have a reputation to uphold.

TRY BEFORE YOU BUY

Before rushing out to buy a canoe, investigate opportunities to "test-drive" several canoes. If you have a friend who will loan a canoe, great. More likely, you'll turn to canoe rental shops, called liveries, which offer a low-risk way to try before you buy. Canoes can be rented for $25–50 per day, sometimes discounted for multiple days or nonpeak times. This is very little compared to the large initial investment involved in canoe ownership.

Reluctant paddlers—worried about canoe tippiness, comfort, and safety—can usually be talked into going out on easy water for a day in a rented canoe. Summer camps, college outdoor programs, and other sources of canoe lessons also offer a way to sample canoeing without buying; besides the chance to try canoes for a small fee, you also get paddling instruction.

The chief advantage of canoe rentals is that they're so widespread. Just about every major waterway has a canoe livery where you can rent by the hour, day, week, or longer. Many provide launching and takeout service, so that you handle the canoe only while it's in the water. In fact, renting is so easy that some experienced canoeists prefer to rent on the spot, rather than transport their personal canoes. Others rent because they lack canoe storage space, don't want to lift a canoe, or cringe at the thought of driving at highway speeds with a canoe perched atop their car. Chief drawback to renting? Only limited models are offered—almost all rental canoes being standard-shaped aluminum "one size fits all" types.

A better way to try canoeing before buying is to patronize a canoe dealership that offers "test paddling" of different models. Often, such a store will sponsor a free paddling day on a local waterway, and anyone who shows up can take a turn paddling different makes of canoes. During a test paddle, take a single stroke, then pause and observe if the canoe continues to glide easily. A canoe that glides further with every paddle stroke than a comparable model means a lot less paddling overall.

Compare each canoe with all the other models available. After the glide test, lean outward and see if the canoe threatens to tip—or if it does tip. Be adventurous—you'll never have as secure a backup as you will during a test paddle. Don't forget to try lifting each model of canoe offered, to get an idea of how much weight you can handle—especially for a solo canoe.

BASIC TYPES OF CANOES

Canoes can be better understood if you subdivide them into categories. Two fundamental differences are size (tandem or solo canoes) and deck (open or covered canoes). A tandem, or two-person canoe, can hold two adults, or two adults and one or two small children, or one adult and two children, depending on the canoe's length and width. Tandem canoes are usually sixteen to eighteen feet long.

Growing in popularity is the solo canoe, accommodating one adult or one adult and a small passenger. *Solo* doesn't necessarily mean small, as many solo canoes are in the fifteen- to seventeen-foot range, although longer, wider solo canoes are intended mainly for solo expedition paddling, with the extra length providing increased load capacity. Many couples like the idea of paddling "separate but equal" canoes, rather than always sharing a single canoe with one spouse (traditionally the male) dominating the steering duties. Solo canoes are also great for independent teenagers, or for single parents who don't always have another adult handy to help with lifting. On the other hand, two people can propel a canoe faster and more easily than a single person.

The choice between open or covered canoe is simple. Covered canoes are strictly whitewater craft. They resemble kayaks more than canoes, except that they use a single-bladed paddle and the paddler kneels. The canoe is covered, or decked over, with the same tough material as the hull construction, forming a watertight compartment inside where the paddler kneels. A spray skirt fastened around the paddler's waist excludes splashes, so the canoe won't fill up with water. River canoes appear tippy but become more stable when put into the current.

PARTS OF A CANOE

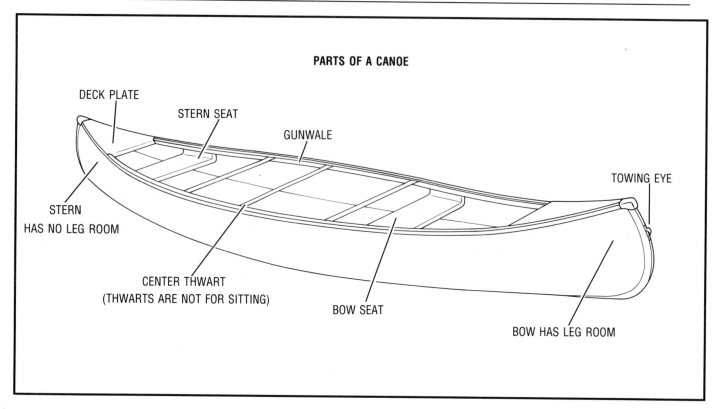

DECK PLATE

STERN SEAT

GUNWALE

TOWING EYE

STERN
HAS NO LEG ROOM

CENTER THWART
(THWARTS ARE NOT FOR SITTING)

BOW SEAT

BOW HAS LEG ROOM

A TANDEM, OR TWO-PERSON, CANOE.

The covered canoe, or C-1 (canoe for one) can be "Eskimo rolled" upright after a tip, like a kayak, and requires a high degree of skill plus upper body strength to master. Another whitewater canoe, called a C-2, is simply a covered canoe designed to accommodate two paddlers.

Open canoes are more versatile, tackling flatwater and big lakes, and if rugged enough for whitewater may be easily rigged to handle spray (see Chapter 7).

CANOE CATEGORIES

Canoe types can be further divided into categories according to their shape and function. The recreational or "all-purpose" canoe, appealing to first-timers, is usually sixteen to seventeen feet long. Traditionally, this is a canoe designed to be steady and safe, yet with some maneuverability. The flat bottom minimizes that teeter-totter sensation. A good width for the recreational canoe is around thirty-four inches, with the depth averaging fourteen inches, plus a little rocker for easier pivoting. The canoe needs to go in a straight line, because beginners have the most trouble with this.

The sitting area is generous enough for comfort, and there should be enough initial stability to permit paddlers to stand up, to cast a fishing line or just to stretch. Such canoes work well for moderate paddling, as most beginners don't need or want the super efficiency of a racing canoe. All-purpose canoes try to be everything to everybody—actually their major drawback, because no canoe can perform well on all kinds of water environments.

The most popular materials for these all-purpose canoes are fiberglass and Kevlar, because of the better designs available for the type of paddling done (on lakes and smooth rivers, these designs make paddling easier and more efficient), and because these materials offer good

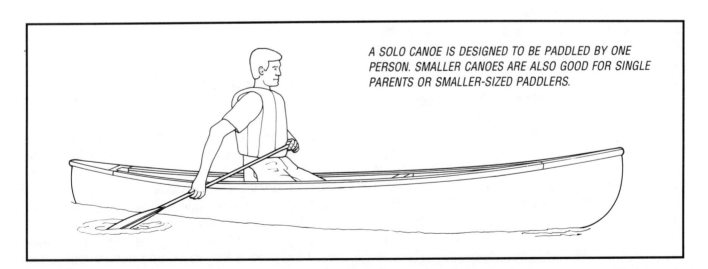

A SOLO CANOE IS DESIGNED TO BE PADDLED BY ONE PERSON. SMALLER CANOES ARE ALSO GOOD FOR SINGLE PARENTS OR SMALLER-SIZED PADDLERS.

abrasion resistance (to resist damage caused by dragging the boat over gravel bars, or other abuse often inflicted by beginners). Aluminum is also favored for its relatively moderate cost and good durability.

A touring canoe is longer—seventeen to eighteen feet—with a sleeker shape—maybe thirty-three inches wide—and deeper to hold gear—more than fourteen inches. This canoe glides fairly easily, with sufficient space for camping gear and food. Canoes with a touring designation should track straighter with less effort. An expedition canoe is the touring canoe's big brother, a canoe with a deeper hull for heavy loads. Expedition or "tripping" canoes have tough hulls and stable designs to handle rough water and withstand the abuse of wild rivers. Besides the weight of two paddlers, a tandem expedition canoe should boast a carrying capacity of at least three hundred pounds.

Cruising and racing canoes are very responsive, but demand skill to handle, like a temperamental racehorse. Canoes built for speed are very long and lean—seventeen to eighteen feet, thirty-two inches wide or less, not more than twelve inches deep—design characteristics that limit stability and capacity. They're mostly for competition (racing) or exercise (cruising), as the narrow shapes are too tippy for general canoeing.

Again, whitewater or river canoes can be open or decked over, with open canoes far better for occasional trips away from rapids—flatwater, camping, etc. Look for a sturdy hull that resists rock damage, a shape that sheds spray, lots of rocker for maneuverability, a depth of fifteen inches, room in front of the seats for kneeling in rapids. Length isn't as important—maybe sixteen to seventeen feet. Shorter, sportier whitewater canoes may be described as whitewater "play boats," specially designed for quick pivoting and "surfing" in river rapids.

On the fringes of the all-purpose canoe are multipurpose boats built even wider, with more step-in stability. Designed to appeal mainly as a low-cost alternative to standard fishing boats, these canoes may sport square sterns or other nonstandard canoe designs.

Finally, there are specialized performance canoes—custom designed for experienced canoeists—plus hybrids that defy categorization. If traditional canoe shapes, materials, and applications don't excite you, consider a hybrid. Most of the basic canoeing techniques are the same, regardless of the boat type you choose.

Don't anguish too much over selecting the perfect canoe. As you've seen, no one canoe fits every need. Keep in mind that canoeing is supposed to be fun. Visit boat shops, talk with people who know canoeing, let your needs be known, test-drive and experiment with canoes before buying, ask questions. Remember that even if you do acquire a canoe that proves unsatisfactory, you can recover most of your investment by reselling it.

TYPES OF HULL MATERIALS

First, and fundamental, canoe choices must be what kind of material the hull, or outer casing, will be constructed from. This will determine how much money the canoe costs. Today, canoeists can sample an assortment of materials as well as construction techniques: wood, aluminum, fiberglass, Kevlar, or plastics. Most traditional materials have gone the way of the buffalo, but a few die-hard canoeists still build their own birchbark canoes, and a few more may spend a winter carefully piecing together a cedar strip canoe.

Whitewater canoe (open style), left, and whitewater kayak, right.

Covered canoe or "C-1." Note that paddler kneels and uses single-blade paddle, unlike kayaker.

CONSIDERATIONS FOR CHOOSING HULL MATERIALS

1. *Durability.* How long will the material hold up, especially if stored outdoors?

2. *Strength of material and construction techniques.* How well the canoe resists rock bashing. Some canoes can even bounce back from being wrapped around a boulder! Also, how stiff is the material? A canoe with lots of reinforcing ribs and thwarts is likely to be made from a flexible material. Stiffer canoes handle better.

3. *Resistance to ultraviolet light.* The sun's rays emit UV, which can crack paint, or weaken and deteriorate hull materials. Sunlight is hard to avoid, too.

4. *Weight.* There are heavy materials, medium materials, and light materials. A seventeen-foot canoe can weigh as little as thirty pounds or over eighty pounds. Generally, the lighter the canoe, the more it costs. But light canoes aren't necessarily flimsy.

5. *Cost.* What is your budget? How serious about canoeing are you? While you aren't under any pressure to buy the best at any cost, the cheapest canoe isn't a bargain in the long run if you can't enjoy it or get a good resale price. Plan on spending more money for a good design and quality workmanship. The extra satisfaction and value derived from a better canoe will be well worth those additional dollars.

6. *Design limitations.* Not all materials can be shaped into the latest designs, and some materials can be used to construct only limited designs. This imposes limitations on handling characteristics of less flexible materials.

7. *Maintenance.* Do you have time and energy to devote to a canoe during the off-season? Or do you want a canoe that can be tossed aside in the backyard and forgotten until spring?

8. *Ease of repair.* Fixing a canoe in the middle of the barrenlands is a challenge regardless of type or materials. On the other hand, a strong canoe won't need to be repaired very often.

9. *Aesthetics.* This is color, how a design looks in the water, eye appeal—important if you are to feel proud of your boat and use it a lot (although ugly canoes are not necessarily hard to handle). Consider also such factors as: How long until sunlight fades that pretty color?

10. *Flotation.* Is it built in, or will you have to take special care to add flotation later?

ABRASION VERSUS IMPACT RESISTANCE

Also consider the difference between a canoe that is abrasion resistant (holds up during repeated dragging over concrete boat ramps and sand bars and in other regular use) or one that is impact resistant (bounces off rocks in whitewater conditions). Many canoes that are abrasion resistant are not impact resistant, and vice versa. Synthetics like fiberglass boast more impact resistance than aluminum, for example, but are more prone to abrasion. Look for a skid plate on the underside of the bow for additional abrasion

Underside of a canoe bow shows the "skid plate," a protective coating that reinforces the area of the canoe often damaged by beaching or dragging the canoe.

aluminum is practically maintenance-free. A business with fifty canoes in service can't be constantly sanding and painting each one. The initial cost for a good aluminum canoe is relatively moderate, so the livery can afford to buy lots of them. They boast good all-purpose designs, essential when renting to a variety of canoe users. They're very durable, with excellent abrasion resistance. UV rays have no effect on aluminum—they're tops in longevity. (This is the canoe of choice for a boat left to winter over at a vacation home.) Resale values are high. Most models are very safe and stable, with excellent carrying capacity, great for expeditions.

Of course, aluminum canoes have their drawbacks. For starters, they're notoriously noisy, cold to sit in, heavy to lift, and just generally "clunky." Even waves slapping against the side of an aluminum canoe produce annoying echoes, detracting from the serenity of canoeing. Also, aluminum sticks to rocks rather than sliding over them, dangerous in rapids. The shiny surface bothers some—not only does the canoe reflect glare, but it gathers heat. "Sometimes I feel like I'm a piece

resistance (or plan on adding one yourself) with fiberglass and Kevlar canoes. Also, any canoe will last longer if exposure to abrasion and impacts is reduced. Lift, don't drag the canoe, whenever possible. Dodge rocks rather than paddling into them.

ALUMINUM

This sturdy metal is the most frequently used material in canoe building. Nearly all liveries rent aluminum canoes because aluminum offers so many advantages over other materials. Most important,

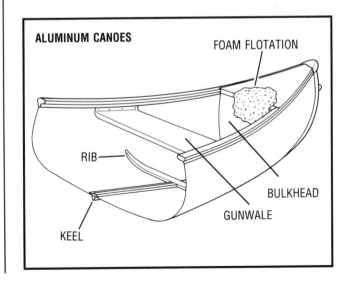

ALUMINUM CANOES

FOAM FLOTATION

RIB

KEEL

BULKHEAD

GUNWALE

of bacon in a frying pan," complains one canoeist.

Since the material is difficult to shape, aluminum canoe designs are always limited. Aluminum favors a fundamental flat-bottomed design—wonderful for casual renters, but not so great for serious boaters. Repairs can be frustrating, too. Aluminum canoes dent, rivets work loose or shear off. Welding can't be done in the field or at home—it requires a shop specializing in aluminum welding. Also, rewelding aluminum can destroy the metal's temper in high-stress areas.

Aluminum canoe production soared after World War II, when manufacturers supplying aluminum for warplanes found themselves with lots of material left over. Canoes made from aluminum were vastly more durable than the only other kind at the time, wood and canvas. The new aluminum canoes quickly gained popularity, overwhelming their rivals. In forming most aluminum canoes, the manufacturer shapes the material over dies in half sections, then rivets the two halves together. Next, the bottoms are reinforced and joined with aluminum ribs. Because of this piecing process, aluminum canoes usually have well-defined keels, which may or may not be desirable.

A few models are made in one piece. If you choose a pieced canoe, select a model with closely spaced, flush rivets. This usually indicates better workmanship. Spot welding is considered by many to be less durable than riveting, and at any rate is harder to repair when damaged. An aluminum canoe's weight depends on how thick the metal skin is; the heavier the hull, the more durable it will be.

If you choose an aluminum canoe, beware of poorly made models. Buy from a reputable manufacturer, and watch the weight. To cut down on cold, place carpet scraps or closed-cell foam pads on the bottom of an aluminum canoe. Attach rubber strips to gunwales to silence paddle bang.

Apply wax to the bottom for improved gliding over rocks.

FIBERGLASS

Fiberglass offers the greatest selection of hull designs available, due to the ease of shaping this material. Many good performance canoes are made from fiberglass or its expensive cousin, Kevlar. Fiberglass is a composition of plastic resin reinforced with glass fibers. Layers of fiberglass cloth—with stronger canoes having more layers—saturated with resin are fitted to a mold and bonded with resin to shape a tough shell, then allowed to dry or "cure."

There are countless production techniques for fiberglass canoe hulls. By experimenting with different "layup" combinations of resin and glass, manufacturers have invented a multitude of fiberglass hulls, and of course each claims to have the best. Some even trademark name materials, such as We-no-nah's "Tuf-weave." Polyester is the most common resin, because it is less expensive and less toxic than other resins. So many variations exist that quality can vary widely. Your best bet is to look for a handmade fiberglass canoe from a small company. Beware of fiberglass canoes that are very inexpensive—these employ "chopper guns" rather than hand work for layups, resulting in poorer quality.

Besides design variety, fiberglass hulls are favored for their moderate strength combined with fairly light weights. Abrasion resistance is also good, and fiberglass is very easy and inexpensive to repair. It's more brittle than aluminum, and can break or crack if hit hard. However, fiberglass does make a quiet hull that, unlike aluminum, tends to slip over rocks rather than stick to them.

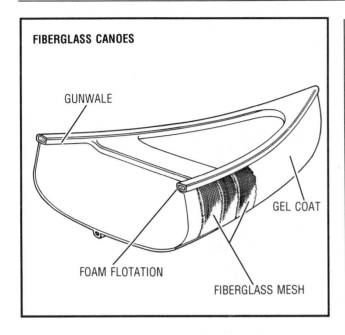

FIBERGLASS CANOES

GUNWALE

GEL COAT

FOAM FLOTATION

FIBERGLASS MESH

KEVLAR

Du Pont's Kevlar 49 is a high-class hull material—similar to fiberglass, but much stronger and lighter—that creates the Cadillacs of the canoe world. Originally developed for use in racing canoes, Kevlar is now available in many other models. Hulls made from Kevlar are incredibly strong for their weight—keep in mind that Kevlar is also used in bulletproof vests, which must be light enough for police officers to wear all day, besides stopping bullets. Kevlar is at least 40 percent stronger than the best fiberglass (but don't try to shoot your Kevlar canoe!).

The chief disadvantage is cost. Kevlar construction is very labor intensive, with much hand work, which in turn means high prices. However,

almost all Kevlar construction is of the highest quality—the material and techniques being too expensive for "economy" manufacturers. Again, as with fiberglass, look for many layers of cloth and resin with fiber reinforcements. A combination of Kevlar and fiberglass offers a good compromise—stronger than fiberglass, less expensive than all-Kevlar.

Because Kevlar utilizes the flexibility of fiberglass, many sophisticated contours and fine designs have emerged. For overall performance, canoes from Kevlar can't be beat. And for the lightest canoe possible—that still retains good strength—Kevlar is the ticket. If you choose Kevlar, though, be sure to store the canoe out of the sun, because UV rays can break down the material.

WOOD

Despite the demand for synthetics, the wood canoe survives. Wood is the overwhelming winner in the aesthetics department, combining a striking appearance with a graceful feel in the water. And wood canoes are not as fragile as they appear. Yet the wood canoe is hardly a beginners' boat. It can't survive banging into rocks or being dragged around like a tough plastic canoe.

Wood canoes are expensive because of the hand labor involved. Strip canoes are made of red or white cedar, covered with fiberglass. Other wood canoes may be made from mahogany or ash. But few manufacturers make wood canoes these days. Still, there is much satisfaction in building your own cedar strip canoe. Wood canoe owners are craftspeople, whether or not they built their boat, because of the continuous, time-consuming maintenance required. Owning a wood canoe is a labor of love for the serious canoeist who cares about canoe heritage.

PLASTICS

Canoe manufacturers like to give special names to their brands of plastic: Royalex, Ram-X, Crosslink3, Oltonar, and so forth. Royalex, for example, is Uniroyal's thermoplastic laminate, while Oltonar is canoe builder Old Town's "exclusive version" of Royalex. Then Crosslink3 is Old Town's "patented rotational molding process" for polyethylene, while Ram-X belongs to camping equipment giant Coleman.

Hype aside, the best plastic canoes can all be termed composites or laminates—their hulls are made from layers of closed-cell foam and ABS plastic. Good plastic canoes are constructed from many layers—an outer vinyl skin, sublayers, core material, more sublayers, then an interior vinyl skin—all sandwiched together to form a tough hull with plenty of built-in flotation. Heat and pressure work to bond the layers tight.

Cheaper plastic canoes are made of polyethylene pellets first heated and pressed into sheets, then vacuum-molded into canoes, without the foam core and its extra flotation. The problem with these thinner plastics is that they're too flexible. Craft made from polyethylene alone do make suitable starter canoes because of their lower cost, but for a tougher canoe, look for multiple layers with a foam core, which creates a stiffer boat, besides adding flotation. Plastic canoes made from polyethylene or ABS with foam cores are rugged enough to survive even deliberate abuse like being dropped off the roof of a building.

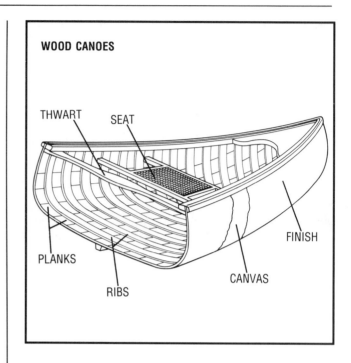

WOOD CANOES

THWART
SEAT
PLANKS
FINISH
RIBS
CANVAS

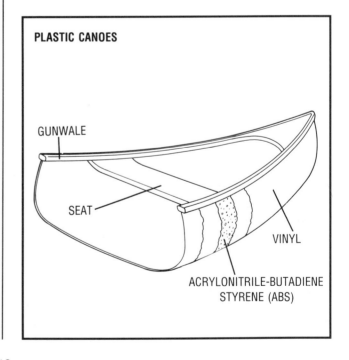

PLASTIC CANOES

GUNWALE
SEAT
VINYL
ACRYLONITRILE-BUTADIENE STYRENE (ABS)

Advantages of good plastic canoes are bright colors, sleek shapes, buoyancy that's built in (with foam core designs), structural memory and resilience (the ability to bounce back to original form after denting), good impact and abrasion resistance, quiet and warm hull material, moderate cost, good strength, plus advanced designs not possible to shape from polyethylene. Royalex creates great whitewater canoes because of its durability and resilience. Many whitewater canoes are made of Royalex or related materials. Good plastic canoes possess an amazing ability to slither over rocks that would stop any other canoe.

Drawbacks depend on the type of plastic and construction method chosen, and may include hulls heavy for their size, difficult repairs, UV deterioration, and good-looking economy models that aren't much of a bargain in the long run. Some plastics weigh as much as aluminum, yet may be preferable because of other characteristics, like the increased variety of hull designs. Others require costly molding equipment to produce, thereby jacking up the overall cost of each canoe built. Prices for plastic hulls are moderating, though, and many people looking for a tough canoe with a responsive design choose plastic.

BASIC HULL DESIGN

Canoes don't just sit on the water. When floating, they displace water. How much water is moved aside depends on the weight of the canoe and load. When the canoe is moving, rather than merely skimming the surface, it pushes water aside. After the canoe's disturbance passes, water fills in behind. During this process, the canoe's hull interacts with the water. How efficient this interaction is depends on hull shape. With a poorly designed hull, paddlers have to work harder than necessary. Obviously, the most efficient hulls are found on racing canoes—if you're competing in the Olympics, you want a canoe design that gives you the edge.

No hull does everything well, but if you have a certain interest, look for a hull shape that does what you want your canoe to do. Otherwise, look for the lines of an all-purpose boat.

One overrated hull feature is the keel—a quarter-inch to two-inch protrusion along the bottom of a canoe, stretching from bow to stern. Many experienced paddlers avoid these external keels because they catch on obstacles, and don't have much effect on keeping the canoe headed straight, despite popular belief to the contrary. For tracking, the overall design of the hull matters more. Keels resist turning, impeding maneuverability. However, a keel can help resist wind. Usually, though, keels exist for added strength in construction, rather than performance.

LENGTH

Choose a length to suit your needs, but bear in mind that longer canoes are actually easier to paddle, more stable with the same load, capable of carrying heavier loads with less loss of performance; they track better, move faster, and glide farther with each stroke for greater efficiency with less effort. Especially on lakes or other calm water, go for a long streamlined canoe rather than a short boat more suited to negotiating hairpin turns.

Beginners often fear that a larger, longer canoe will be harder to handle, when in fact the reverse is true. Beginners have the most trouble getting a canoe to go straight. Here, paddling a longer canoe helps. Yet most canoes labeled as all-purpose canoes, designed with beginners in mind, are shorter than they should be. With a shorter canoe, you have to exert more energy to make it go forward. This is why the seventeen-foot length is easily the most popular size of canoe. The difference between carrying a fifteen-foot canoe and carrying a seventeen-foot canoe isn't all that great. Remember also that weight and price are governed more by construction than size.

Shorter usually does mean lighter, less expensive, less cumbersome, easier to load, and quicker pivoting, especially with a solo canoe. The most important virtue of a short canoe is sharper turns. A short hull is good for small people or kids, and for paddling on tight streams. Otherwise, look for length. Even solo canoes aren't all that short. And, be careful you don't visualize a canoe in the store as too long without a realistic perspective: Most canoes fit on any car.

Longer canoes—18 to 18.5 feet—handle surprisingly well with two people paddling, especially if they want to carry lots of gear. Even bigger canoes are sometimes encountered, but these are special designs: freight canoes, for floating heavy loads, and "war canoes" that carry up to a dozen kids or more—lots of fun at summer camp, but not practical for the average household.

BOW SHAPE

A pointed nose, or end, allows the canoe to slice through water, producing less resistance for more speed. Canoes with sharp tips will be speedy on flatwater, and will track better, besides creating a sleeker appearance. Conversely, a blunter, more

buoyant nose rides over waves, good for negotiating whitewater, besides increasing carrying capacity. A snubbed end also resists impacts, a good feature in busy rapids. Some materials—aluminum and plastics—require construction methods that limit bow shape designs. The bottom (water-side) portion of the bow can be square-shaped, for better tracking, or rounded, for easier turning.

TELLING BOW FROM STERN

At first glance, many canoes appear symmetrical, with matching ends. However, a closer look reveals small differences in the interior design that differentiate the bow, or front, of the canoe from the stern, or back. Often, manufacturers place their name, or the canoe's model name, on the bow. More reliably, with a tandem canoe, look at the seating arrangements. The bow seat provides leg room in front to accommodate kneeling. Just the opposite, the stern seat has an obvious lack of leg room behind it, forcing the paddler to sit or kneel facing forward.

WIDTH

A primary function of width—or "beam"—is the addition of stability. However, a wider canoe isn't necessarily more stable under all conditions (see Cross Section). Very wide canoes are often vaunted as superstable multipurpose boats ideal for fishing or general beginner use, and they do have appeal for the nervous novice because of

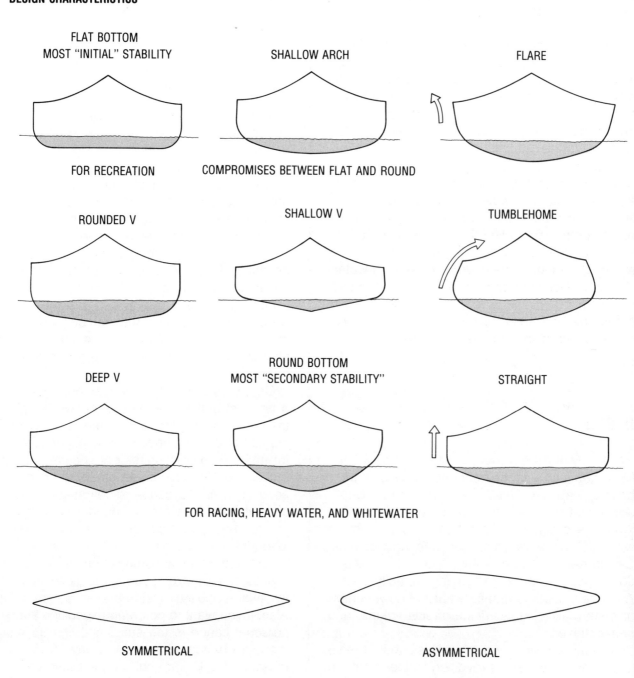

DESIGN CHARACTERISTICS

FLAT BOTTOM
MOST "INITIAL" STABILITY

SHALLOW ARCH

FLARE

FOR RECREATION

COMPROMISES BETWEEN FLAT AND ROUND

ROUNDED V

SHALLOW V

TUMBLEHOME

DEEP V

ROUND BOTTOM
MOST "SECONDARY STABILITY"

STRAIGHT

FOR RACING, HEAVY WATER, AND WHITEWATER

SYMMETRICAL

ASYMMETRICAL

that initial reassuring steadiness. But some handling ease is sacrificed for that extra width, and the canoe doesn't work as well in current.

Additional width also adds to carrying capacity, yet not as much as length. A long hull holds more and performs better loaded. Canoes that are too wide aren't as efficient, because their wide hulls push more water, requiring more work with the paddle. Canoes were originally designed long and lean for a reason, so don't get one that's too wide.

Width is measured between the gunwales, at widest point, and the maximum at the waterline. A canoe's width at waterline exerts the most influence on how it handles. Canoe width should be the proportion to length and purpose. For example, a professional racing canoe would have a twenty-seven-inch beam at the three-inch waterline; a competition cruiser has a thirty-two-inch minimum beam at the four-inch waterline mandated by the U.S. Canoe Association; wilderness expedition canoes can be wider.

DEPTH

More depth in a canoe generates additional freeboard, capacity, and seaworthiness. Depth doesn't affect tracking, speed, or turning. But there are problems with too much depth—more wind resistance, which causes steering problems. Canoe depth is particularly important in expedition canoes where extra carrying capacity is vital. A canoe's depth is measured at the bow, center, and stern. The center depth affects volume and seaworthiness.

A shallow canoe would be less than twelve inches deep, while an expedition canoe might run fourteen inches or more. More depth also keeps a canoe drier through waves.

WEIGHT

Whether you select a featherweight thirty-pound solo canoe for its ease of handling off the water or choose to struggle under an eighty-pound aluminum canoe depends again on how you use a canoe, plus your canoe budget (remember that making a good canoe that is also lightweight costs more). In the canoe world, a ninety-pounder is considered a very heavy canoe. Eighty pounds is more average, with seventy being light, and anything fifty pounds or less borders on flimsy, unless the construction is Kevlar.

Lightweight canoes are mostly sturdy, but beware of weak canoes that tempt you with low prices. Don't sacrifice good construction for a few pounds. Ask about hull strength before you succumb.

On the other hand, if you plan on tandem paddling most of the time, two people will be dividing the weight. Consider your partner, too—even lifting half of a really heavy canoe might be difficult for a slightly built youngster or spouse. If moving the canoe always creates stress, then the purpose of owning a canoe is defeated—you won't get out onto the water as often if your canoe is just too heavy and cumbersome to load and unload all the time.

Here's another advantage rentals offer—most liveries employ strong young people to lift canoes for their paddling customers all summer long. Also, if you want to go on an expedition and your personal canoe is too small and light to handle the extra baggage, you can always rent a more muscular boat, often right at the put-in site.

ROCKER

A canoe's rocker is the curve along its keel line—how much the bottom of the canoe is flat and sitting in the water, how much is curved up above the water. Think of a rocking chair's supports to remember what rocker looks like. Rocker allows a canoe to pivot or spin around. Canoes with extreme rocker turn on a dime but don't track well, while canoes with little rocker go straight without performing turns very well. Most paddlers compromise between no rocker and extreme rocker.

The rockered hull performs like a shorter boat because of the shorter waterline. Boats with extreme rocker are great for slalom racing, navigating tight streams or tricky whitewater. On the other hand, a marathon racing canoe would have no rocker at all, because the goal is straight-ahead speed. Canoe rocker usually ranges from 1 to 5 inches, with the average being around 1.5 to 2 inches.

CROSS SECTION SHAPE: TO V OR NOT TO V

Imagine slicing a canoe through the middle, and you arrive at a cross section shape, a design feature that reflects how stable and safe a particular canoe will be. Some canoes feel stable when you first step into them—the flat-bottomed canoe—but become tippy when you try technical maneuvers like brace strokes, in which the canoe is

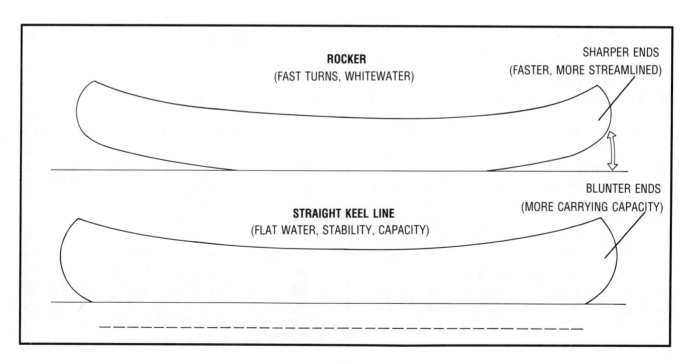

ROCKER
(FAST TURNS, WHITEWATER)

SHARPER ENDS
(FASTER, MORE STREAMLINED)

STRAIGHT KEEL LINE
(FLAT WATER, STABILITY, CAPACITY)

BLUNTER ENDS
(MORE CARRYING CAPACITY)

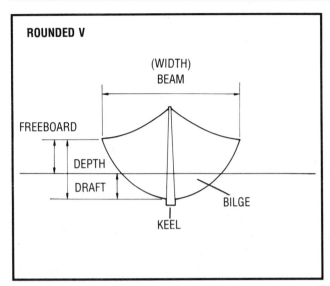

ROUNDED V

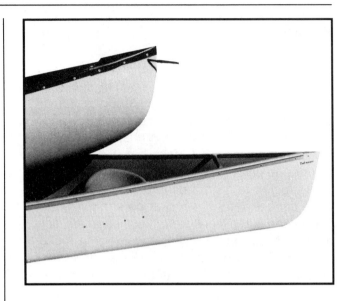

Top canoe is rockered, bottom canoe has flat keel line. Note "grab loop" on top canoe for whitewater use.

heeled over. So there are really two kinds of stability to consider: initial and secondary. Initial stability is steadiness when you first step into the canoe, while secondary (or final) is ultimate resistance to tipping over.

Canoe bottoms range from flat to round. A flat-bottomed hull seems steady when level, but can tip over very suddenly in wild waters. The opposite is a round bottom, which feels very tippy at first, requiring the paddler to adjust, rather than just sit and paddle. This rounded bottom is good in whitewater, and speedy for racing, but requires skill just to keep right side up on flatwater, somewhat like a kayak.

For canoeists tackling many different water conditions, the best "slices" to consider are the modified round V or shallow arch types, a compromise between initial stability and control over a canoe's unpredictable behavior. These shapes are better at speed and tracking on flatwater than the flat bottom, besides handling moderate rapids. If you are very concerned about stability on flatwater, though, the flat bottom may be preferable.

TUMBLEHOME AND FLARE

While the bottom of a canoe's "slice" plows through the water, the upper part stays dry, except during vigorous activity. Then—especially when you are paddling whitewater—a hull's upper shape assumes importance. Think of the canoe slice as the letter *C* lying on its left side. If the tips of the *C* bend inward, the hull has tumblehome. If the tips curve outward, that's flare.

Outward flare at the top of a canoe helps deflect waves and resist capsizing, important for a whitewater canoe. Flare does force you to reach further to paddle, which can be awkward for beginners.

Tumblehome is simply the reverse of flare. It's a design feature often used in solo canoes, as

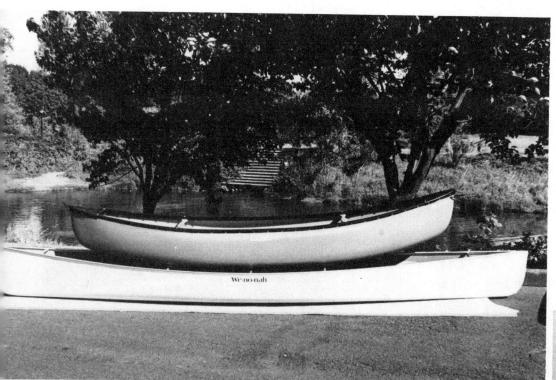

The top canoe has rocker, good for quick turns and negotiating whitewater.
The bottom canoe has a flat keel line for flatwater paddling.

Note the rocker in this whitewater canoe. Having paddlers sit closer together also gives more lift to bow and stern.

this reverse flaring allows paddling close to the hull, which is necessary to keep the solo canoe on a straight course. Some canoe designs feature a combination of tumblehome with slight flare, to have the best of both worlds.

CANOE INTERIORS: SEATS, GUNWALES, THWARTS

There is more to a canoe than just the hull. What's inside counts, too. Most canoes arrive with bare-bones interiors, leaving customization up to the individual. But what you can do with a canoe is limited by the basic interior design. You usually can't, for example, remove a thwart that gets in your way. So take a good look at the canoe's furnishings before you make any decisions.

Gunwales (pronounced "gunnels"), those rails around the top outside edges of the canoe, need to be strong. You will be putting your weight on them, plus they take a lot of abuse during loading, transporting, and carrying.

Many canoeists prefer wood gunwales, for the good feel that wood offers. Wood is easy on the hands while lifting and carrying the canoe, besides being less noisy than other materials. However, wood gunwales can require special care that the rest of the canoe doesn't. Aluminum gunwales are tough and don't require upkeep, but are less aesthetically pleasing, in addition to sounding off whenever a paddle strikes them.

Check for gunwales that have smooth edges, rather than sharp protrusions—these are much easier on the hands and paddles. Gunwales should have a good, solid feeling, not flimsy or flexible, because they contribute to the strength and rigidity of a canoe.

The type and placement of seats affects not

A comfortable, springy cane seat.

only comfort, but also the stability and strength of a canoe. Seats in a canoe should be low enough to keep paddlers' center of gravity low, without being so low that they're awkward or don't permit the feet to be tucked underneath if desired. Low seats help to keep your weight low in the boat even when you're sitting. However, seats should allow kneeling when desired—or when necessary. Because heavy gear placed in the canoe's bilge makes any hull more stable, low seats are more important when paddling an empty boat.

You will spend a lot of time on the canoe seats, so choose a design that suits your anatomy. Canoe seats can be flat metal, sculpted bucket-type seats, springy woven cane, or wood. Check seat placement for paddlers' leg room and comfort. Of course, you can always add to the canoe seats' comfort by using foam pads, but there will be times when these are forgotten, lost, or just not bothered with. Then you're stuck with the seats you chose.

Check to see that canoe seats are securely mounted to the hull, and watch out for hanging seats that may swing or wiggle—these are not as strong as other seat arrangements.

Another consideration is what kind of custom seats can be added to the canoe model you're considering. A paddler who needs or wants lower back support, for instance, might favor a canoe that has auxiliary seats with backrests, or at least a way to rig something. A paddler who is considering whitewater will want a canoe with seating that permits the addition of a saddle or custom kneeling pads. Special sliding seats that accommodate different canoeing positions, or different-sized paddlers, are available, but might not fit your canoe. An advantage of sliding seats is that they allow you to trim (balance) the hull without moving gear around. It's much easier to move seats than gear.

Bear in mind that all interior additions like gunwales and seats add more weight to the overall canoe. Check the canoe's listed weight first to determine if add-ons are included, or if the weight is that of the hull alone. This additional weight depends on the type of interior additions (wood trim is heavier than aluminum trim). Those fancy sliding seats are nice to have, but they do make the canoe heavier.

Another interior feature to look for in a canoe is built-in flotation. Some canoes have sealed compartments or air pockets that keep the canoe afloat even when swamped (full of water). In rapids, an overturned canoe will need to float higher to avoid banging against submerged rocks. Whitewater paddlers usually add flotation or covers to be sure. However, even if you stick with flatwater paddling, flotation is important for the added safety and security—you won't be stranded out in the middle of a lake if your canoe always floats. Sealed gear bags that displace water also add to flotation.

CARRYING CAPACITY

This is one canoe characteristic very likely to be overstated by an unscrupulous manufacturer. Also, carrying capacity—how much weight a canoe can safely transport—varies so much that setting a specific limit for a canoe can be difficult. Some manufacturers don't give suggested carrying capacities for this reason. And vague limits don't help—a canoe that can carry "three adults" may not be able to carry three very large adults, or even two large adults.

Body weight is usually known, but most canoeists don't make a habit of weighing their equipment before loading. How, then, to decide on carrying capacity? A beginner should look for a generous load capacity, because more skill is required to handle a heavily loaded canoe. Think about what kind of trips you plan. If you are mostly interested in short trips, or aren't really sure yet, a canoe with less carrying capacity will probably work fine. A big clunky freighter isn't the best choice for starting out, unless you have your heart set on paddling the entire Yukon River. And a large-volume canoe can always be rented for an expedition, especially in canoe country.

Whatever your canoe's carrying capacity, it's prudent to always have your canoe loaded below official limits.

CANOE HYBRIDS

An interesting variety of canoelike craft have surfaced in recent years, reflecting the strong growth of paddling as sport and recreation. There have always been canoe hybrids designed with fishing or hunting in mind—wider, with more initial sta-

A kayaklike hybrid boat, paddled kayak style.

bility, shorter than traditional canoes, often with a square stern for easier motor attachment. Besides providing a solid platform for casting a line, these hybrid canoes cartopped easily, and accessed far more water than standard rowboats or johnboats ever could.

Now there are kayaks that look more like canoes, long and narrow inflatable canoes, and multipurpose boats. With a multipurpose boat, you have a "hardshell" boat (rather than an inflatable) that easily adapts to rowing, sailing, and motoring. Traditional canoes can do all three as

well, but certain designs work better—after all, canoes were built for paddling. These multipurpose boats have more interior space, with comfortable seating, because of their extra width—more like a rowboat or sailboat than a canoe. Of course, when the boat gets bigger than a canoe, it also becomes heavier. But if you envision a boat that won't be paddled most of the time, these multipurpose craft may better suit your needs.

Contributing to the overlap between canoeing and kayaking are the folding kayaks, which

Inflatable canoe paddled while kneeling, with double-bladed paddle.

closely resemble old-fashioned canvas-covered canoes; sea kayaks, which are long and narrow like canoes; and sit-on-top kayaks, mostly for ocean surfing but cropping up everywhere. Traditionally, kayaks are distinguished from canoes by their double-bladed paddle; paddlers sitting down with legs out front, rather than kneeling or sitting with legs bent; and height (canoes have more boat above the water). Distinctions between kayaks and canoes are blurring, which is not necessarily bad. Rather than worry about whether a particular boat is a canoe or kayak, or what kind of paddle to use, boaters should concentrate on what kind of boat suits their needs, and which positions and paddles work best for them in their boat of choice.

THE INFLATABLE CANOE

Inflatable canoes follow the success of their predecessors, the inflatable kayaks. These just-add-air boats soared to popularity chiefly because they're extremely easy to paddle. While paddling a traditional "hardshell" kayak often took months to learn, beginners could jump into inflatable kayaks and start paddling right away, even through serious whitewater. Now canoeists can enjoy the benefits of owning an inflatable boat, if they choose.

Inflatables offer a new twist to the grand tradition of canoeing. At last, there is a canoe that you can easily store in your apartment, and transport in the trunk or backseat of your car. Deflated, an inflatable takes up less room than a suitcase. Once at the launch site, an inflatable canoe can be pumped up within five minutes, using a foot or hand pump, or an electric-powered pump that operates off a car battery. Inflatable canoes are more forgiving of mistakes, bouncing off rocks that would tear open the toughest hardshell canoe. The design of most inflatables increases stability, eliminating that tippy feeling when you first climb aboard. Inflatables are safer for novices in rapids, because technique isn't as important—the boat gets you through. Kneeling on an air mattress-type floor is comfortable, even during a long day. Inflatable canoes make great whitewater playboats, allowing even the most timid beginner an immediate start in surfing waves, riding holes, and eddy hopping. A bonus: They handle shallow-water conditions very well, too.

Good quality inflatables last for years, plus they're made of tough fabric that resists damage, yet is a cinch to repair. Look for multiple air chambers (at least two, better to have three) for additional safety, and strong valves (one-inch military-style valves of metal or sturdy plastic, rather than air mattress–style plugs). Most important is the base fabric used for the "hull" of an inflatable, combined with a coating to seal air inside and resist UV rays (much as a fiberglass canoe is made of cloth and resin). Neoprene, Hypalon, or PVC coatings over strong nylon or polyester fabric are the best.

Beware of unreinforced PVC inflatables—"vinyl"—beckoning from the aisles of discount stores. These are little more than toys that can be useless, even dangerous, on a wild river or in the middle of a big lake. Sturdier fabrics with a good coating are necessary for a canoe that will respond to the paddle. Unreinforced vinyl inflatables are floppy rather than rigid. They catch wind, turn sluggishly, sag under the pressure of whitewater. Use them only on more sheltered waters.

Surprisingly, the major drawback to inflatables is their high price. Quality inflatables involve a lot of labor, such as hand-sealed seams, and this attention to construction costs more. Good coatings like Hypalon are expensive. Plus, inflatables are a specialty item. They aren't mass-produced for the multitudes, like aluminum canoes. Only a select group of paddlers choose the inflatable canoe, but that is changing.

Also, all inflatables are horrible in wind—they never handle as well as hardshell boats against a breeze. Inflatables are at their best in a current, or with the wind behind them.

You may wonder about the differences between inflatable kayaks and canoes, since many canoe paddlers use a kayaker's double-bladed paddle for propelling their inflatable canoe. Usually, though, the inflatable canoe is longer and wider, with blunted tips. These blunt tips keep the nose from diving into river hydraulics, a plus for whitewater playboating. Canoeists also kneel for greater power in rapids. Overlap exists, however, so now we have inflatable sea kayaks, which are long and narrow like canoes, and Pack Cats or Paddle Cats, which are two inflated tubes joined by a seat, more like a raft than a canoe. If the idea of an inflatable canoe interests you, do some research so you can decide if the inflatable is the boat for you, and if so, which type of inflatable suits your needs.

CHAPTER 3

THE WELL-DRESSED CANOEIST: NECESSITIES FOR PADDLING

Once you have acquired a canoe, only three basic accessories are mandatory to start having fun. These are a set of paddles, life jacket or PFD (personal flotation device), and a way to carry the canoe, usually a roof rack. Later, you can add items for comfort, such as seats with backrests, or equipment for advanced paddling, like flotation bags and wet suits. In the beginning, though, there's no need for the complications and costs of gadgets.

CHOOSING THE PROPER PADDLE

The paddle provides the connection between canoeist and water. As it is the basic tool used to control the canoe, selection is important. A poorly made paddle, or one that is the wrong size, will make paddling harder, detracting from your canoeing enjoyment.

For starters, two different implements move a nonmotorized boat: oars and paddles. Oars are long, thin poles without end grips and are used in pairs by a single rower (oarperson) to control a boat. The motion is called *rowing*. Paddles, on the other hand, have shorter shafts with end grips and are used singly by a paddler. This motion is known as *paddling*. You can't paddle with an oar or row with a paddle, although many people confuse the two. Despite the versatility that allows a canoe to be rowed, paddles are almost universally employed to propel a canoe.

Paddles are available in two basic materials—

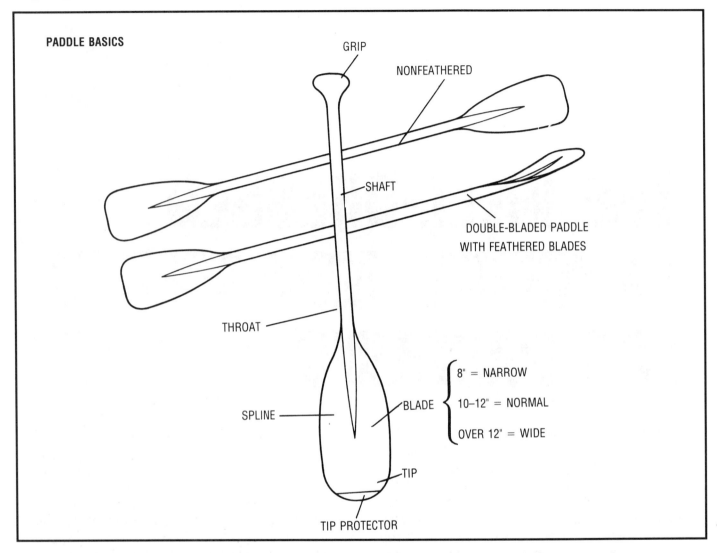

PADDLE BASICS

GRIP

NONFEATHERED

SHAFT

DOUBLE-BLADED PADDLE
WITH FEATHERED BLADES

THROAT

SPLINE

BLADE

8" = NARROW

10–12" = NORMAL

OVER 12" = WIDE

TIP

TIP PROTECTOR

wood or synthetics such as aluminum—and two fundamental designs—single-bladed or double-bladed. Traditionally, canoeists have used only single-bladed paddles, while kayakers claimed the double-bladed paddles. However, traditions are changing fast. Many canoeists have discovered the efficiency of the kayaker's paddle. Old-fashioned canoeists may balk, but the double-bladed paddle has proved its worth in the canoeing world, especially in the solo canoe. It's handy, also, for parents of younger children who need more control of their canoe than immature paddlers can provide, and for propelling canoe hybrids. For starters, though, the standard single blade is easier to learn and more practical in a tandem canoe.

First, consider a paddle's length. Traditional methods of holding a paddle up to your chin, then

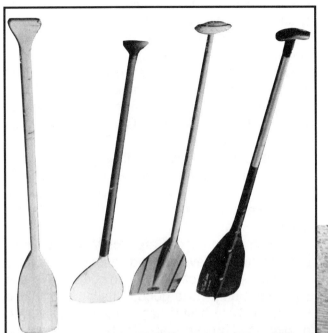

Four different paddle styles. From left to right: basic wood, synthetic, bent-shaft wood, synthetic. The left paddle has an awkward pear-style grip (often found on cheaper wood paddles), the paddle on the far right has a T-grip, the middle paddles have versions modified for comfortable graspling.

The paddler in the stern prefers a long paddle for better reach and power in turns.

fine for lake cruising, but river paddling demands shorter-shafted paddles with wider blades for increased power against the current. However, canoe racers prefer longer paddles.

Try the on-water measuring technique: Sit in the canoe seat, then submerge the paddle blade completely. The top of the grip should be at shoulder level. Consider, also, that most adults don't vary much in torso size. Three-quarters of all adults can use a standard fifty-four-inch paddle that has a thirty-four-inch shaft and a twenty-inch-long blade. Or, sit in a chair and measure from your nose to the sitting surface (for shaft length only).

Though wood canoes are mostly history, wood paddles still find favor among canoeists. Paddlers prefer wood for appearance and comfort. A wood paddle not only looks good, it feels good. Wood is less likely to blister hands than synthetics. A quality wood paddle is also lightweight, lessening fatigue, yet strong to resist cracking or breaking under stress.

An overwhelming advantage of the synthetic is minimal maintenance. Wood paddles must be sanded and varnished occasionally, and are more prone to warping (though cheap synthetics can warp merely from the force of plunging them into water). Plus, costs for a good synthetic paddle, constructed of plastic over aluminum, are lower than for a quality wood paddle. Synthetics also are reasonably lightweight as well as durable.

Avoid cheap wood paddles—they are usually fragile. Look for ash or maple woods, not fir or pine, or quality laminates that combine hard and soft woods. Heft paddles before buying, so you don't get stuck with one that feels like lead. Remember, the lighter the paddle, the easier it will be on your body after a full day of paddling. Also avoid shabby synthetic paddles available in discount stores, especially those that look more like

Canoeing instructor demonstrates the correct way to use a bent-shaft paddle, with the "elbow" toward you.

selecting one that length or a few inches shorter, just aren't all that accurate. Paddle length depends more on your torso size—the distance from shoulder to hip—and how long your reach is, in addition to what size and kind of canoe you have and where you are sitting. The stern position usually requires a longer paddle than the bow, and a solo canoeist usually prefers a longer paddle as well. Also consider where you will be paddling. The chin-height paddle may work just oars—without grips—and those that must be assembled before use.

Canoe paddles come with either a T-shaped or rounded end, known as the paddle grip. A T-grip paddle is most efficient for moving a canoe, particularly in whitewater, while the pear-shaped grip is more comfortable to hold for longer periods. It's highly impractical to use a paddle lacking a good, solid grip, because grips increase your leverage, letting your muscles work more efficiently with less effort. If there are any rough edges on a paddle's grip, smooth them down before using the paddle. Smooth surfaces help avoid blistering.

Although your synthetic paddle may someday resemble the canoe racer's bent shaft—after a close encounter with a rock—learning to use a bent-shafted paddle may prove worthwhile. The bent shaft allows a more efficient stroke for cruising and racing (but not in rapids) by remaining vertical through most of the paddle stroke. It's not hard to learn unless you're accustomed to a straight shaft. Hold a bent-shaft paddle with the "elbow" of the bend *toward* you.

Blade width also affects how a paddle handles. Although narrow blades are less efficient, they're easier to handle and control. A wider blade catches more water, increasing efficiency of each stroke, but also requires greater control. Even a mild current has sufficient force to grab on to a wide blade, to the point of yanking the paddle from the hands of an unwary paddler. A narrow paddle blade is eight to ten inches wide; medium is ten to twelve inches. Broader yet are "beavertail" paddles that deliver plenty of power for canoeists with the experience to handle them, especially in rapids. Blades can be rounded, rectangular, or square, with total surface area determining efficiency—the more surface, the greater the force a paddle can exert against the water.

A paddle's weakest spot is the blade tip, the part most likely to strike rocks. Tips of laminated wood paddles must be reinforced with a strip of hardwood or other durable material. All paddles last longer if blade tips are protected by metal or rubber reinforcing strips, available already installed or as add-ons.

Your paddle needn't be expensive—a good, serviceable synthetic will run around twenty dollars—and will last for years with proper care. Besides installing a protective cover for the blade tip, treat the paddle with respect. Don't let it dangle when not in use. Never use a canoe paddle to push off rocks or the river bottom. Don't waterfight with your paddle, as the force of slapping water at an angle can warp less durable paddles quickly. Always take a moment when loading or unloading to place paddles in a safe area so they don't get stepped on or driven over. At home, store paddles hanging up if possible. If you have several paddles, make or buy a rack to hang them by the T-grips.

Don't forget that you need a paddle for each canoeist, plus a spare in case one is lost. You might want to have one regular and one bent-shaft paddle for variety. And even the youngest child will want to have his or her own paddle to help out, if only for a few minutes. Children's paddles must be lighter as well as shorter, but bear in mind that kids' shorter arms sometimes need more reach.

Balance and feel of a particular paddle are more difficult to determine. Each person has his or her own preferences, which can be determined only by experimenting with different kinds and lengths of paddles.

THE DOUBLE-BLADED PADDLE

We've seen that the double-bladed paddle is not just for kayaks. More canoeists are using them all the time. Especially for a hybrid canoe like an inflatable, a double-bladed paddle increases efficiency. Yet a basic problem with double-bladed paddles is that nearly all are built with kayaks in mind. Kayaks are narrower and shorter than canoes, so paddles are shorter. In a canoe, you'll need a longer reach. Look for paddles offered to inflatable kayakers, which are longer because these boats are wider than standard kayaks, or for sea kayaking paddles (though blades tend to be narrower). A double-bladed paddle needs to be eight or nine feet long to successfully propel most canoes.

Look for a paddle that can be set with blades either "feathered" (with one blade at a 90-degree angle to the other) or unfeathered (both blades flat). This offers more versatility in paddling. You may also want a double-bladed paddle that breaks down into two pieces. Although the central joint makes the shaft somewhat weaker than a one-piece paddle, the convenience of storing and transporting two pieces is worth the sacrifice. For beginners, choose a double-bladed paddle without spoon, or curved, blades, which are more difficult to master. Using the double-bladed paddle requires some extra effort, but the increased efficiency will please you. Even if you plan on using regular canoe paddles for all of your paddling, borrowing or renting a double-bladed paddle for a day might prove interesting. Take one along on your next canoe outing and see how it works for you.

THE PROPER PFD

Equally important as paddles are life preservers, known as personal flotation devices or PFDs in canoe terminology. Every canoeist must have a life vest and should always wear it. Even good

Canoeists prefer Coast Guard Type III PFDs, especially this "shortie" style, which offers full freedom of motion.

swimmers can be surprised by a dunking in cold water, and swimming through whitewater without additional flotation is foolhardy. Frothy rapids offer little buoyancy for a swimmer. With today's attractive, stylish PFDs, there's no reason not to wear a life jacket all the time while canoeing. At the minimum, all nonswimmers, whitewater boaters, expedition trippers, and children should always wear PFDs. Like safety belts, PFDs don't work if they're not fastened, so don't just throw them into the canoe. In case of upset, just locating a PFD can prove difficult, besides the problem of pulling it on while in the water.

The best PFD for canoeing is the Coast Guard Type III rated vest. This PFD offers maximum protection with minimal restriction on freedom of motion. Canoeists need generously cut armholes to allow rotation of shoulders during paddling. PFDs rated Type III usually feature foam ribs that flex with the paddler, increasing range of motion. Most Type IIIs have a minimum buoyant force of fifteen pounds, sufficient for flatwater and most canoeing rapids. Each person must try on a PFD and select one that fits snugly, yet is comfortable. Type IIIs come in small, medium, large, and extra large, so one vest won't suffice for different people. Best to put your name in Magic Marker on the PFD so that you alone use the vest—then you don't have to keep making size adjustments every time you go canoeing.

The vest must have enough sturdy closures—waist ties, zippers, plastic buckles (avoid uncoated metal)—to keep it from riding up over your head. Practice paddle strokes when trying on a vest, to see if your hands brush against fasteners (this can be painful with metal buckles) or if an ill-fitting vest restricts movement. Expect to pay at least fifty dollars for a good canoeing vest, and consider it money well spent.

Particularly important is proper sizing for children's PFDs. Look for crotch straps to keep the PFD on the child, plus snug ties or zippers. Set an example for your child by always wearing your own vest, and you won't get complaints about PFDs being "nerdy."

Some types of PFDs simply aren't suitable for canoeing. The Type I is a huge, bulky jacket made for extreme rough water conditions, and hampers your movement too much. This is the old navy "Mae West" life jacket—not practical at all. The Type II is known as a "horsecollar" and fits around the head. This, too, is a cumbersome

vest. Don't try to save a few dollars by choosing this cheap PFD—you won't enjoy wearing it. The Type IV is a float cushion, designed for throwing to a swimmer. Problem is, if the canoe has overturned, these are out of reach and there is nobody to throw them. Use float cushions only for kneeling pads (this they do wonderfully).

Many whitewater rafters use specialized Type V PFDs, but these are full vest styles, more restrictive of movement than the Type IIIs. However, they do perform well in extreme whitewater, so if you're floating the Colorado River through Grand Canyon in your canoe—or similar big water—they might be worth considering. Special "hi-float" jackets in this category contain up to thirty pounds of flotation, a lifesaver if you are swimming huge waves. (Keep in mind that a Type V doesn't satisfy the Coast Guard requirement for a PFD unless it is actually being worn.)

One PFD growing in popularity among boaters is the "squirt" vest, a minimal jacket with fifteen pounds of flotation that is very stylish. Squirt vests are favored by whitewater "rodeo" paddlers for freedom of movement created by careful foam insert placement.

To help your PFD last longer, don't use it as a kneeling pad, backrest, seat cushion, or sleeping pad. Never use it to pad a canoe while cartopping. When traveling, keep PFDs inside or stowed in a bag to protect them from wind damage or being blown out of the vehicle (which happens often due to their light weight). Follow the manufacturer's recommendations for washing the PFD, avoiding harsh chemicals that could damage the flotation foam inside. Hang your life vest up after each use so that it dries without mildewing, but not in the sun—that encourages mold spores. In camp or at the boat ramp, the moment you take the PFD off, clip it to a thwart or tree so it doesn't blow away. Also, because many life vests look alike, and aren't cheap, keep an eye on them at crowded launch sites. You'll want to have your address and phone number, besides your name, written in waterproof felt marker so the vest can be identified as yours.

ROOF RACKS

Once you own a canoe, you need to be able to get your new boat to the water. Roof racks are the most popular, and easiest, method for transporting canoes, although you can use a trailer, or put a short canoe into the bed of a pickup truck. Just about any car, even a compact model, is capable of carrying a canoe. Many novice canoeists are nervous about cartopping their canoe, but with a few sensible precautions, there's no need to worry—thousands of canoes travel safely every day. Keep in mind your vehicle's new, higher clearance with a canoe on top (measure for complete peace of mind). And make sure the canoe is always well secured before driving off. Check lashings after traversing bumpy railroad crossings or bad roads. Slow down in windy conditions.

For that first trip home from the store, you may be supplied with blocks of Styrofoam or similar material. These work well for shorter trips at slower speeds, offering a cheap, easy, immediate alternative to a roof rack. Position the canoe first, centering it over the car, then slide pads to front and back edges and secure with ropes or straps. Or, should you find yourself with canoe and no roof rack, rig a temporary setup by using thick foam pads or folded blankets to pad your car's roof where the gunwales of the canoe make contact. This works for short distances if you drive carefully.

For longer trips at highway speeds, you'll need

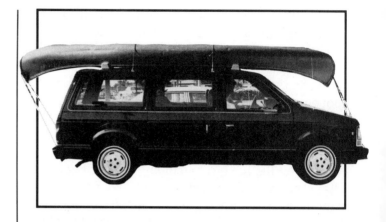

Carrying a canoe on a car roof with foam blocks. Note bow and stern tie-downs.

a more substantial roof rack. Check your car's rain gutters—some newer cars don't have the substantial weight-bearing gutters required to install some roof rack designs. A basic canoe rack consists of two crossbars with four clamps. The clamps secure the bars to the roof. The canoe is lifted up to the rack, centered, then lashed down. Or make your own by purchasing four gutter clamps, then attaching two-by-fours.

With more sophisticated roof racks, such as the Yakima system, you can use one rack to carry a bicycle or skis in addition to canoes. Also, the design permits gear to be locked down to the rack, and even allows the rack to be locked to the vehicle for total security while traveling or parked on the street.

TIE-DOWNS

Gone are the days when cartopping a canoe required the knot-tying proficiency of a Boy Scout

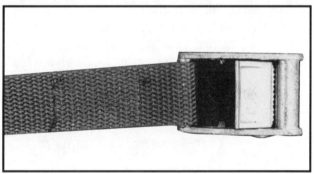

Cambuckle straps, like those rafters use, offer a great alternative to knots and ropes—fast and easy to fasten.

Rope remains the traditional tie-down. Make sure the rope you select is strong and of the right length—avoid excess lines or straps allowed to flap around in the breeze. Useful knots for canoe cartopping are the trucker's hitch and the tautline hitch, knots that can be tightened or loosened without undoing, perfect for securing bow and stern. A canoe should be fastened down with a minimum of four lines: one each on bow and stern, plus two across the middle. Stretchy bungee cords work well for the middle tie-downs. Attach bow and stern lines to the car's bumper—these lines provide additional security for high speeds, long-distance driving, and wind gusts. Best for strength is an inverted V on bow and stern. Check to make sure rope edges aren't chafing against rough spots on the bumpers. Some canoeists use S-hooks to avoid abrading ropes.

Test the canoe after fastening everything, making certain it's tight and won't slide around, a prime cause of abrasion damage. With more than one canoe, pad the space between them with scraps of carpeting.

PAINTERS

Experienced canoeists attach two ropes to their canoe, one to the bow and the other to the stern. These lines, known as painters, are left fastened to the canoe at all times, with the free ends coiled away (best secured with a piece of inner tube rubber or bungee cord) when the canoe is paddled. Painters are perfect for cartopping, while also serving as tie-downs at the boat dock or in camp, as a way to pull the canoe along shore, or for self-rescue. Check painters often for weak, fraying spots that could break unexpectedly. Rope for painters should be polypropylene floating line.

plus the vocabulary of a sailor. Rope can be avoided altogether by using durable nylon webbing with heavy-duty cambuckles—the kind of straps popular with whitewater rafters. If you don't trust your knot-tying capabilities, then straps offer a fine alternative. They don't jam and are easy to tighten or loosen. Straps are available through whitewater equipment suppliers, by mail order if your area doesn't have a retail store.

TRAILERS

Most trailers used in canoeing carry many canoes at once, designed to accommodate liveries or canoe outfitters. If you anticipate carrying several canoes, a trailer with "shelves" for stacking may prove useful. Such a trailer usually has to be custom-built for you, unless you can locate a used one (not uncommon in canoe country). Also, on some vehicles, several canoes may be stacked together on the roof rack.

A narrow trailer, such as the kind employed for transporting a johnboat or rowboat, can also move a single canoe. A big advantage in trailering your canoe is that the canoe never has to be lifted. This appeals to the disabled, and to seniors and other people who can't lift a canoe as high as a car's roof rack. Trailers also work well for heavy canoes. With a roll bar, simply slide the

bow of the canoe forward and the rest will follow easily. Adding a winch makes the process practically effortless. If the waterway where you're headed has a boat ramp, when you arrive, just back the trailer down into the water and let the canoe float off.

With all this ease of operation, of course, comes the major drawback: learning how to handle a trailer. Trailers add another complication to the simplicity of canoeing, but the effort required may be worth the independence from lifting a boat. Your vehicle needs a compatible trailer hitch, a hookup for trailer lights (check these often to make sure they still work), and sometimes a trailer license (consult state regulations). You'll also require safety chains for backup attachment between trailer and vehicle, plus you may want to lock the trailer onto the hitch.

Practice maneuvering your trailer in an empty parking lot before you hit the highway. For the most part, a narrow canoe trailer follows the tow-

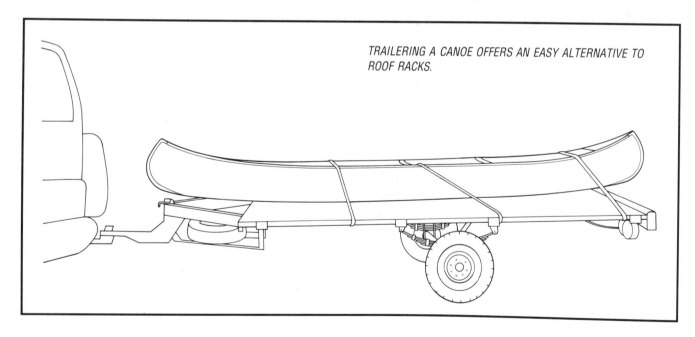

TRAILERING A CANOE OFFERS AN EASY ALTERNATIVE TO ROOF RACKS.

ing vehicle nicely. Problems arise when attempting to back up the trailer. Here, it's helpful to remember that the trailer moves in the *opposite* direction of the steering wheel. For instance, if you wish to back the trailer to your left, turn the steering wheel to the right. Veteran truckers employ this trick: steer with one hand, gripping the six o'clock position on the steering wheel. Then just turn the wheel as you normally would, and the trailer should follow. Don't attempt backing down a crowded boat ramp until your trailering skills are polished. And, for safety's sake, always give warning when backing up a trailer.

CANOE CONTAINERS

Even on flatwater, canoes tend to collect a little water inside. And loose things can blow away or otherwise get lost overboard. The bottom of a canoe is no place to leave small items lying around—you risk stumbling over things, or stepping on the camera. You'll need to protect your supplies with water-resistant containers. These assume important roles when tripping down rivers, where spray seems to go everywhere, and on overnight expeditions, when food and sleeping gear must be kept dry.

Special bags and boxes, available from canoe equipment suppliers, will keep your things safely stowed and away from water. Dry bags are available in all sizes, from small sacks that snap on to a thwart to giant Duluth expedition packs that allow you to portage a hundred pounds of backcountry supplies. Most bags are made of heavy-duty PVC material with a roll-down top and straps to hold the top closed, while some are urethane-coated nylon, which is tougher. Velcro fastenings add to a dry bag's security. Sealed bags will float,

and add flotation to the canoe, but most canoeists prefer to tie them into the thwarts for peace of mind.

The Duluth pack is a special gear carrier designed and constructed specifically for transporting in the bilge of a canoe. Canvas is the traditional material, but nylon is gaining in popularity because it sheds water and resists rot. Don't try to use backpacks in your canoe, because the frames will hang up on thwarts, seats, or gunwales. Most Duluth packs feature a tumpline—a headband that transfers weight while portaging—for carrying heavy loads more efficiently. Use plastic abrasion liners like heavy-duty garbage bags inside the packs for additional security.

A bag is only as watertight as its closure, so take the time to close the bag properly. Squeeze excess air out first, then fasten all the bag's straps. Also, be gentle with your dry bags to avoid damaging them, which causes leakage. Don't throw them on the ground, set them down. Don't use dry bags as sitting pads or ground sheets. When traveling, make sure the bags aren't being chafed by tie-down ropes or buckles. Carry a patch kit for the dry bags.

For short trips, you can get by with improvised dry bags. Line a pack with a garbage bag, for example, and load things into this inner lining. Small items can be put into self-sealing sandwich or freezer bags, then stowed in a small pack that is clipped on to a thwart. A vacuum sealer comes in handy for waterproof-sealing small items, like a change of socks, and especially for sealing food items.

Cameras and binoculars, as well as wallets and keys, deserve extra protection. An army surplus ammunition can is perfect. Strap or tie the can into the canoe. If you carry cameras often, line the box with closed-cell foam to pad delicate equipment. Inflatable camera bags offer protection without resorting to a clunky can. Test such waterproof containers first, at home in the bath-tub, before entrusting your valuable gear to them. Bear in mind that no container will be waterproof all the time. Insure your valuables against damage before tripping; consult your insurance agent about extending your homeowner's policy to cover canoe trips as well as traveling to and from canoe trips.

Money and keys are best carried in a fanny pack attached to the waist, or stored in a water-proof clip-on bag for wetter trips through whitewater. (It's smart to have a second set of car keys around, stowed separately, just in case.)

Larger, dry storage boxes, kitchen boxes, and coolers can hold items that don't fit into bags. When selecting containers, consider where your canoe trips are going—if you'll need to portage a lot, heavy boxes will be more difficult to carry than dry bags or canoe packs that have padded shoulder straps attached. At the other end of the scale, use an assortment of little bags and pouches, fastened to thwarts or under seats, for things you need accessible yet safe: maps, sun lotion, midday munchies.

COMFORT ITEMS

After you've spent some time playing with your canoe, you will know what parts of the canoe need padding or other improvements for comfort. Most desirable are kneeling pads to protect knees from a canoe's hard bottom. Standard float cushions work well for this purpose, or you can acquire special sculpted pads designed to be permanently installed. Some canoeists prefer strap-on knee pads like those for gardening.

Flat canoe seats can get hard after a full day of paddling, and most don't come with back sup-port, so cane seats are popular additions. Those float cushions work for behinds as well as knees. Folding canoe chairs, which accommodate passengers in the middle of a canoe, can be removed for use around camp or at the beach. If sitting unsupported bothers your back, add a cane seat or try one of the new foam back supports sold by outdoor equipment retailers. Some canoes come equipped with sculpted bucket seats, which are quite cozy, while others have flat hard seats and definitely require custom cushioning.

Some folks swear by canoe carts, wheelbar-rowlike contraptions that allow the canoe to be walked around. If you really hate portaging, you might want to give one a try (one version allows towing a canoe by bicycle). Again, though, you are looking at more stuff plus greater expense.

Knee pads glued inside for permanent comfort. Note D-rings in front of pads.

Most comfort items are small additions that really make a difference, so don't hesitate to "complicate" your canoeing experience a little beyond the basics. Anything that adds to your enjoyment will prove worthwhile.

CLOTHING FOR CANOEISTS

Just starting out, you won't need any special clothing. Dress for the weather. Try to begin canoeing on a day when the weather is perfect, so you can go in shorts and T-shirt. Then add storm gear to your canoeing bag so you don't have to worry about being out in the rain or wind.

Even on flatwater, you can get splashed while canoeing. You'll want to have a change of clothes for each person, in case someone does get wet. On a short trip, leave these in your car. For a longer excursion, always pack a bag of extra clothing to take along.

Avoid cotton—jeans and sweatpants are the worst offenders—as much as you can when canoeing. Cotton stays wet all day, and wet cotton robs the body of heat. In moderate weather, it's better to wear shorts and let bare legs dry than to be in wet jeans. A good rainsuit—both top and bottom—is worth acquiring for canoeing. This keeps you dry through the spray of small rapids as well as in drizzly conditions.

Fleece outerwear is fine for canoeing. A fleece sweater wicks away moisture, and always looks good, even after three days of camping out. Fleece pants offer total luxury during cold weather trips, insulating your fanny from a cold canoe seat. It's especially important that kids stay warm when canoeing. Kids love wearing fleece, so you don't have to nag about jackets as much.

Wool and polypropylene are also good fabrics for canoeing outfits.

For expedition travel, each person should have a warm jacket or parka, preferably with a hood; raingear and windgear (wearing good raingear all the time wears off the waterproof coatings); warm hat (stocking cap) and gloves; wool socks; warm camp shoes and water-resistant canoe shoes.

Leather boots with rubber bottoms are popular with canoeists. Or wear wool socks with old tennis shoes when wading. In really cold weather when you must wade, wetsuit booties come in handy. If you just can't keep your feet warm, use a simple vapor-barrier system: Place bare feet directly into plastic bags, pull socks over the bags, then place two more bags over the socks. Sounds disgusting, but works great for the truly cold-blooded. Also useful in a pinch is a sprinkle of cayenne pepper into shoes or inside socks (but be careful of skin allergies).

When the weather is cold, dress in layers. Start with underwear of polypro, silk, netting, or Capilene that wicks perspiration away from the body. Add shirts, fleece tops, pants, and jackets. Over this, wear rain- or windgear as necessary. Take off garments, especially above the waist, while paddling or moving around; put them back on while resting. The idea is to avoid chilling the body with sweat.

In warm weather, clothing, especially footwear, becomes simpler. River sandals, Aqua Sox, or similar attire protect feet while wading. Avoid walking around barefoot, or paddling in rocky rapids without secure footwear. Sandals should strap firmly around feet—don't wear thongs except in camp. Bathing suits or shorts are fine, but use plenty of sunscreen. The sun's rays reflect off water surfaces, creating a mirror effect that easily causes burns. Also protect eyes with polarized sunglasses, and wear a brimmed hat to shield the face.

DRESSING FOR SUCCESS

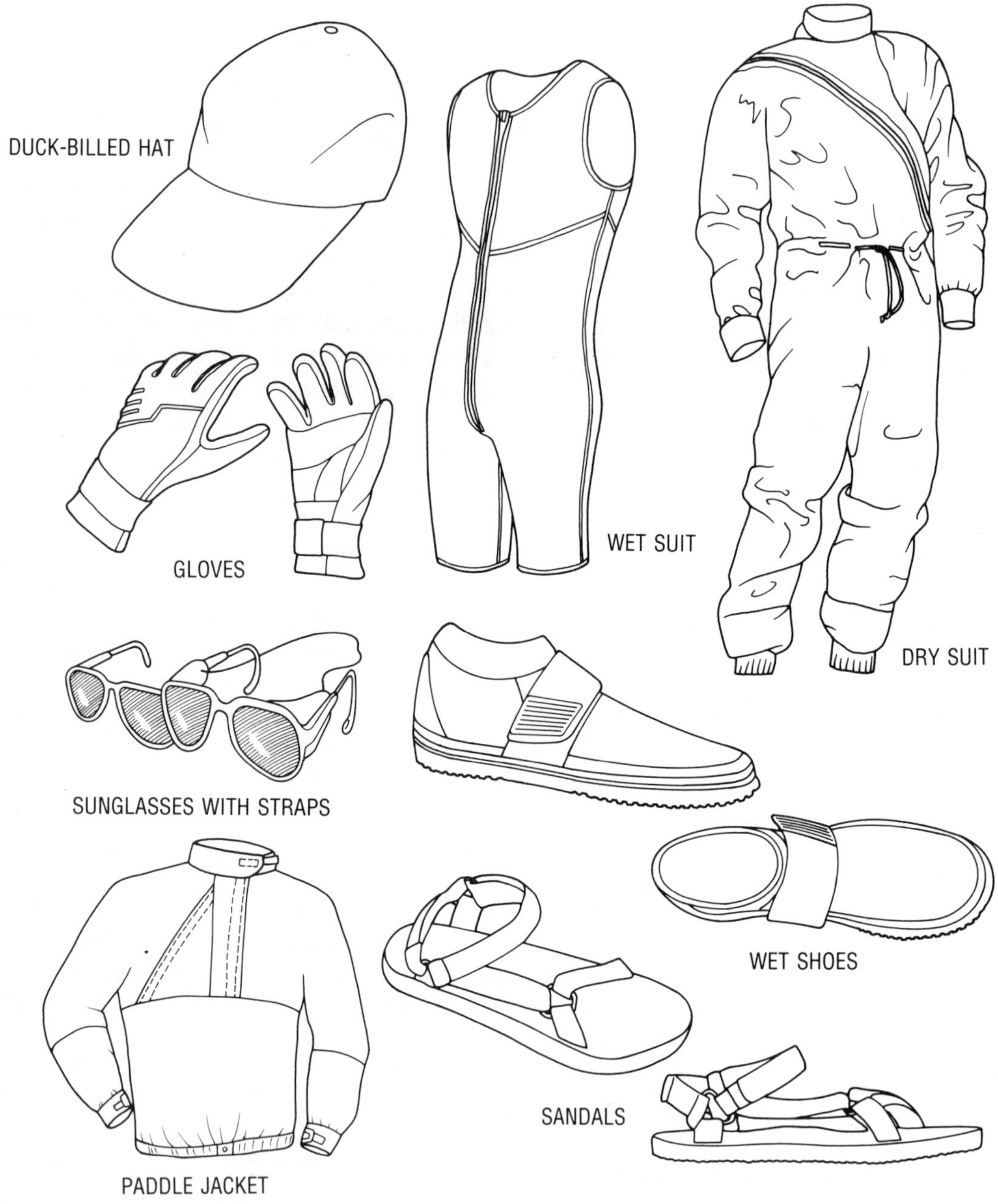

DUCK-BILLED HAT

GLOVES

WET SUIT

DRY SUIT

SUNGLASSES WITH STRAPS

WET SHOES

PADDLE JACKET

SANDALS

When dressing for canoeing, remember that things can be lost overboard. Secure prescription glasses as well as sunglasses with the special straps sold for this purpose—Croakies, Chums, etc.—or buy rubber surgical tubing (from the fishing department) to make your own glasses retainer. Hats need chin straps to keep them on through wind and waves. Leave nonwaterproof watches, jewelry, and other easily damaged items at home.

When camping, you may want a small towel, hiking boots, or cross-training athletic shoes (for exploring on land), plus a few personal items (book, toilet kit, medications, journal, hobby gear, musical instrument).

SPECIAL CANOE CLOTHING

Whitewater canoeing, in particular, demands an outfit that keeps you warm even when doused, yet won't impede motion should you fall overboard. The neoprene wet suit has filled this role admirably for many years. With the upswing in cold-water sports like boardsailing, lots of stylish wet suits are available. Neoprene waders will substitute for a wet suit, but don't wear the rubber hip waders fishermen use. These can fill up with water, making swimming in fast current difficult even with a PFD. For most flatwater canoeing, however, a wet suit is cumbersome, and not necessarily all that warm. Consider that in order to be effective, a wet suit must first be wet. Before that first wave inundates the canoe, the wet suit will be cold. If you don't get splashed at all, you may not stay warm enough. And wet suits offer little protection from chilling winds. But in any situation where a dunking is possible—whitewater in particular—the wet suit offers excellent protection against hypothermia.

Serious whitewater boaters often choose the dry suit, which resembles a space suit without the helmet. If the weather is bitter cold, they wear polypro or Capilene underwear with the suit. By excluding icy river water, the dry suit allows off-season boating in relative comfort. Keep in mind that dry suits are expensive (around $200), somewhat fragile (stay out of brush while wearing one), plus hard to get into (some require a helper to zip the back).

In moderate conditions, a paddle jacket offers a good compromise. This is like a nylon wind shell, except it's sealed at cuffs and neck to exclude spray in addition to wind. With your lower body down inside the canoe, the paddling jacket will keep you warm and comfortable through most conditions, while costing less than a wet suit or dry suit. The jacket can also be worn over a sleeveless wet suit for extra protection. Matching paddle pants can be worn with the jacket, or if the weather is moderate, pair the paddle jacket with shorts.

Many canoeists like to wear special gloves designed to pad the palms where the paddle grip is clutched, a prime spot for blisters. Gloves can add warmth, too, or protect hands from sun and wind. Leather is the most comfortable material for protective gloves, but doesn't work well when wet. Avoid slippery glove materials, such as wool, when paddling. For cold, wet conditions, the best gloves are neoprene, perhaps with the fingers cut out for a better feel of the paddle (available in the fishing department).

THE LITTLE THINGS

You'll want to have a bailer, a container used to ship water out of the canoe, even if you never go near whitewater. Even flatwater waves can splash water into your canoe, and once there, the water just sloshes around until you scoop it out, as unlike some boats, canoes aren't constructed with drain plugs or self-bailing features. Most canoeists construct serviceable bailers out of one-gallon plastic jugs, such as the kind chlorine bleach or vinegar comes in. A small bucket with a handle works well, too. A sponge to mop up spray drops sounds fussy, but comes in handy for keeping the canoe dry. Use a heavy-duty industrial sponge for this purpose.

Before heading out to the backcountry with your canoe, you'll want to put together some kind of repair kit. This should include a roll of duct tape (fixes almost anything from broken paddles to punctured dry bags), material to patch your canoe (depending on what your canoe is constructed from), a compatible adhesive for the material, a solvent if needed, instructions for patching your canoe (these should be provided by the manufacturer, and occasionally a full repair kit is also supplied), any tools you may need (pliers and screwdrivers always prove useful, or add one of the new multitools that are like a super Swiss Army knife with pliers, scissors, and many other attachments), sewing equipment (for fixing clothes, packs, sails, etc.), plus any spare parts (for example, rivets to fix an aluminum canoe). Cold cure epoxy and fiberglass cloth patch just about any canoe in the boonies, working even in wet, cold conditions.

At home, you'll want supplies to keep your canoe looking good and protected from UV rays. This may range from nothing (for an aluminum canoe) to 303 Protectant (good for plastic ca-

noes). Wood canoes and paddles require occasional coats of varnish, with sandpaper to remove old coats.

Eventually, you'll want to have a special storage place for your canoe, probably under cover to protect it from sun, moisture, and rain. Choose a spot sheltered from wind, so the canoe won't be blown around. Brackets may be mounted into the ceiling of your garage, high enough to permit parking your car underneath. The canoe can be hoisted into position using a system of pulleys and ropes. Outside, you can make a rack of two sawhorses or T-shaped braces, or store the canoe on the roof of garage or house, tied down to resist winds. A tarp keeps off rain, sun, and debris

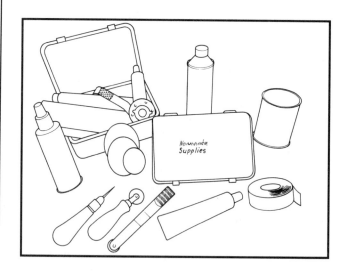

A manufacturer-supplied repair kit, or one that you assemble yourself, will ensure trouble-free paddling.

like falling leaves. You might also want to lock the canoe down, thwart to rack, with a bicycle chain or similar locking device, to prevent theft.

If you store a canoe on the ground or on concrete, be sure dampness won't damage the canoe, and place it open side down so no one is tempted to step in it. Remember that rain and sun can rot wood gunwales. Don't leave a canoe with wood gunwales lying around for any length of time—keep it elevated. The only canoe that can survive being outside all the time, unprotected from the weather, is the aluminum canoe.

CHAPTER 4

PADDLING YOUR OWN CANOE

Before you can use a paddle, you'll need to lift and carry the canoe from storage to roof rack to water. How you handle a canoe out of the water is just as important as your paddling technique. More canoe damage is caused by improper handling on land than by striking obstacles in water! Hoisting a canoe and walking with it takes more technique than strength. Remember that a canoe on land is out of its natural environment. Handle it carefully; never drop the canoe, or let it scrape across anything. Handling a canoe over water minimizes the risk of damaging it, but this means wet feet.

Avoid lifting the canoe by yourself if you have assistance. If solo lifting is necessary, use the one-person lift. First, grasp the center thwart with your right hand as you spin the canoe upward to the thighs. Then use your left hand to grab the top gunwale just ahead of the center thwart, balancing the canoe on your thighs. From here, push your right knee upward, snapping the canoe up and around, over your head. Settle the canoe down on your shoulders. Relax and test the canoe's balance. For the one-person lift and carry, having yoke pads or improvised padding where the shoulders rest against the center thwart is extremely helpful.

Another way to lift a canoe solo starts with lifting one end, sometimes known as an "end lift." Lift and turn the canoe over so the open side is facing toward the ground, and you are standing underneath. Next, work your way further underneath the canoe by placing one hand on each gunwale and walking forward. When you reach the middle of the canoe, bend your knees and hoist the canoe skyward. This lift technique does put strain on one end, which can chafe against the ground, so it's best used on a soft surface like grass, rather than on rocky areas.

As you are learning a solo lift, have another

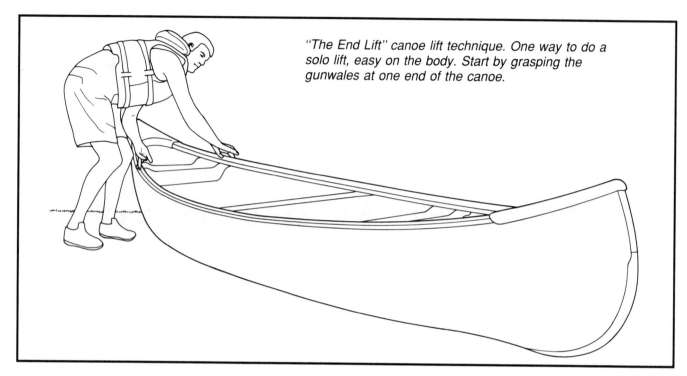

"The End Lift" canoe lift technique. One way to do a solo lift, easy on the body. Start by grasping the gunwales at one end of the canoe.

person assist you while you learn, and develop your balance. He or she helps position the canoe on your shoulders, and stands by to offer aid as you practice walking with the canoe, which takes some getting used to. After a time, you will develop not only your balance and technique, but also your lifting muscles, so that hoisting the canoe feels easier and more natural.

There are lots of ways for two people to lift and carry a canoe. Each person can grasp a gunwale, deck plate, seat, or the underside of bow and stern, then walk in unison, carrying the canoe. Or one person can assist another with a solo lift technique, especially useful for two people of different size and strength.

Lifting a canoe high to a roof rack can prove difficult for paddlers with weak upper body muscles. A stronger or taller partner can hoist one end of the canoe high onto the rack, letting the boat balance with the weaker person

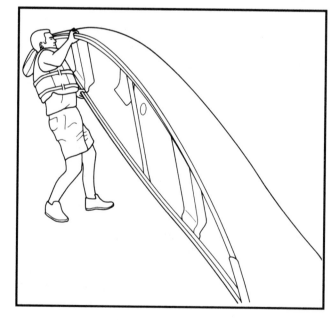

Lift one end up.

48

Work your way to the middle of the canoe, using the gunwales.

Balance the canoe on your shoulders—now you're ready to portage! With practice, anyone can carry most canoes solo!

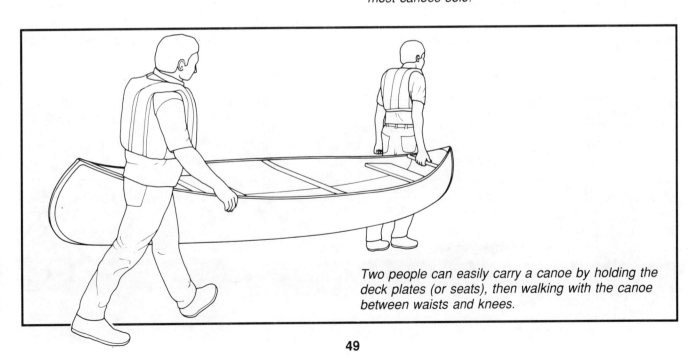

Two people can easily carry a canoe by holding the deck plates (or seats), then walking with the canoe between waists and knees.

holding the lower end. Then the stronger partner leaves the high end and walks to the low end, hoisting and then swinging the canoe around until it's on the rack. Use height augmentation—a ladder, step stool, or overturned bail bucket—as necessary. Just make sure you assume a firm stance on a solid support while lifting a canoe.

To get the canoe down, decide beforehand which side the canoe will be lifted down on, then move together. Bend your knees, hold the canoe by the stems, or ends, on the inside. Slowly lower the canoe toward the ground. Turn upright and set the canoe down carefully. Never drop a canoe.

ALL ABOARD!

At first, your canoe will seem an unstable, even tippy craft, especially when you're attempting to board (get into the canoe). To avoid disgrace right at the launch site, you must employ the correct techniques to stabilize the canoe. For starters, bear in mind that the canoe is designed to

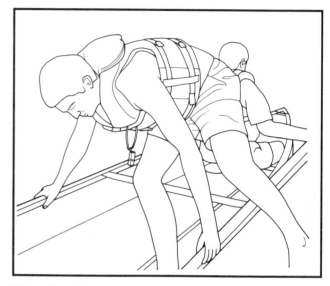

When boarding, center your weight over the keel line. Balance yourself by grasping the gunwales. Once inside the canoe, walk to your position while remaining over the keel line.

carry a load only when completely supported by water. A canoe isn't meant to serve as a bridge. With one end on shore and the other in water, the canoe is vulnerable, besides unstable. You

It's best to hold the stern and load the bow first, because the bow seat is wider, providing better balance.

▲

When boarding a canoe, have your partner hold the canoe steady. And always have the canoe most of the way in the water. For best balance, the stern partner should board last.

When unloading, the stern gets out first, with the wider bow seat again providing balance. Then the stern steadies the canoe for the bow partner to depart.

should never walk in a canoe except when it's afloat.

In a tandem canoe, one partner steadies the canoe while the other boards. Usually the paddler who sits in the back (stern position) braces the canoe while the person who will be riding in the bow (front) position carefully climbs through the canoe from the stern. The bow partner should board first because the canoe is wider at the bow seat than at the stern seat. This wider seat provides more balance. When exiting, follow the reverse: let the stern paddler get out first, while the wider bow seat provides stability.

When boarding, always keep your weight low and centered over the keel line. You can hold the gunwales to balance yourself. The second paddler doesn't board until the first is well settled.

Another way to board, especially in deep water or in a solo canoe, is to position the canoe parallel to shore. Again, one partner can hold the canoe while the other climbs in, then the inside partner can steady the canoe for the second person. Any heavy gear should be placed on the floor in the center (known as amidships position).

You may have heard that you should never stand up in a canoe. This isn't necessarily true. At first, while you are learning to balance, standing up isn't advisable, much less necessary. After you develop confidence in your canoe, however, you can stand up if you like, as long as the canoe isn't moving quickly or otherwise unsteady (such as in a heavy wind). There are good reasons for standing up in a canoe, too: to rest and stretch the legs, for a change of pace, for increased visibility when approaching whitewater, and especially for poling the canoe.

Another misconception about canoeing is that when a couple goes paddling, the man always takes the stern, while the woman sits in the bow. It's true that the heavier paddler usually balances better in the stern, and that the heavier paddler

is most likely to be the male. Traditionally, the paddler in the stern also is responsible for deciding where the canoe is going, and for directing the bow paddler. This can cause resentment, if not outright argument, among couples, as well as between parent and teenager. In the tandem canoe, partners should take turns learning both positions. Even if they decide one person is better at paddling in the stern than the other, for balance, control, or other reasons, there's less room for bad feelings if each fully understands and appreciates both roles.

Among experienced canoeists, it's traditional to place an inexperienced partner in the bow. The stern position allows the experienced partner ample opportunity to observe how the novice is doing, to offer corrective tips, and to call out which strokes on which side the bow partner needs to perform. But the bow partner is important to the tandem team, especially in whitewater. From the bow, obstacles like rocks are glimpsed first, and often it's up to the bow paddler to decide how to dodge these obstacles, or at least to let his or her partner in the stern know about them. The strong disadvantage of sitting in the bow is that the paddler can't see behind without contorting the body.

Whichever position, tandems should never paddle on the same side of the canoe. This will throw the canoe way off course. Paddle on opposite sides, switching occasionally to relieve your muscles and add interest to paddling.

CANOE POSITIONS: TO SIT OR TO KNEEL?

Still another myth about canoeing, which has kept many people from enjoying this sport, is that canoeists must kneel all the time. In flatwater, or

KNEELING

The traditional kneel, holding the paddle by grip properly, hands about shoulder width apart.

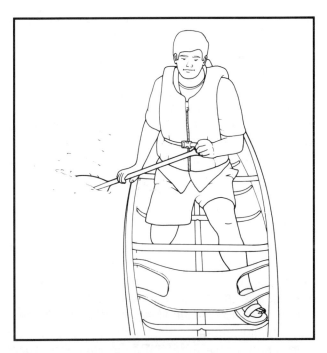

Kneeling on one leg lets the other knee rest. Also good for disabled knees.

whenever balance isn't of utmost importance, certainly sitting on the canoe seats is much more comfortable over the long haul. If constant kneeling were required in canoeing, canoes wouldn't have seats at all.

The truth is that kneeling in canoes for long periods of time is uncomfortable for most people. Canoeists who kneel regularly stretch muscles and toughen pressure points, which allows them to kneel longer with less discomfort. Knee pads take a lot of the sting out of kneeling, as float cushions or cane seats increase the comfort of sitting. Whether you sit or kneel, one way to add stability is to spread the knees wide and press them against the sides of the canoe. And shift positions often to avoid fatigue.

Paddling through whitewater is another matter entirely. Here, balance is crucial, and kneeling down in the canoe adds to balance by lowering

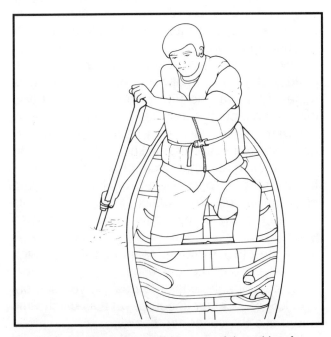

The high kneel position offers powerful stroking for racing or a change of pace.

the paddler's center of gravity. Yet you can fudge on kneeling even in whitewater. For instance, women, who tend to carry most of their body weight low, can often get by with a partial kneel. You can kneel on first one knee, then the other. The position with one knee bent and the other extended works well if the body is wedged against the canoe for stability in rapids. People with disabilities that prevent kneeling, such as a total knee replacement or arthritis, can use this one-knee relief position while tackling whitewater. A person who can't or won't kneel shouldn't plan on paddling extreme whitewater, but moderate rapids can be enjoyed if the paddler is low and braced, and the canoe is well balanced.

And, in serious whitewater, most canoeists employ special supports that make kneeling much more comfortable than you might imagine. Knee pads and float cushions are just a start. There are customized whitewater "saddles" that take body weight off the knees, allowing a paddler to be in the kneeling position all day long without tiring or getting kinked up.

How you position yourself in the canoe depends, at least partially, on how the canoe is rigged. Low seats help keep your center of gravity low, and although they make the canoe feel a bit awkward to begin with, they help stabilize the canoe. Low seats also permit kneeling with the buttocks resting on the edge of the seat, which transfers some body weight off the knees and onto the canoe seat. Watch, though, for seats that are too low for legs to tuck underneath when kneeling.

On the other extreme, seats that are too high definitely unbalance the canoe. They may feel more comfortable, easier to position yourself on, with lots of room for kneeling, yet they catch wind and make the canoe top heavy.

In a solo canoe, many positions are possible, with each offering advantages and disadvan-

Traditional kneeling position in canoe bow.

tages. A preferred position is kneeling amidships, but off to one side of the canoe. This position allows paddling close to the body, for a more responsive canoe. Another solo canoe position is kneeling far enough to one side so that the canoe leans over, almost on edge. This shortens the canoe's waterline, allowing sharp turns. With practice, these positions become more natural, and your sense of balance increases.

A powerful position for racing is the high kneel, with the body high in the canoe. Balance is precarious, but the paddler can throw plenty of force behind the paddle. This is a good position to try just as a variation of sitting or kneeling, especially when you need to make some time across flatwater.

TRIM

Trim means proper balance. This solo paddler demonstrates an obviously unbalanced canoe.

Trim is the way the canoe sits in the water. When a canoe is trim, it's completely balanced. Generally, the bow should ride a little higher than the stern. If the stern rides too deep, the canoe will be harder to steer. Keeping the bow light is fairly easy because most canoes feature bow seats that are set back from the bow tip. The backseats, though, are closer to the tip of the stern. A heavy stern paddler may have to shift his or her weight forward to keep the canoe trim.

However, there are times when you might want to alter a canoe's trim. In waves and whitewater, for example, a light bow is preferable, allowing the canoe to ride over turbulence. When the wind is blowing, though, load the bow down. Most gear is carried amidships (in the middle), and tied or strapped to the thwarts (to prevent loss—it's difficult to lose an entire canoe).

Never use rocks as ballast for a solo canoe. These can damage a canoe. Proper trim in a solo canoe is accomplished by proper positioning in the middle of the canoe. Or, when paddling a tandem canoe solo, add gear bags to the bow. These add ballast safely, and offer a plus of extra flotation.

55

DIFFERENT STROKES

All classic canoe strokes combine two movements: the stroke itself, and the recovery. Both movements are important for proper, effective paddling. Beginners can fudge without noticing much difference, but in the long run learning good form increases efficiency. Poor form spells trouble in advanced canoeing, especially in whitewater situations. If you start out paddling the right way, you won't have any bad habits to overcome.

You don't need to know dozens of strokes to start enjoying canoeing. The basic strokes described here are plenty for most casual paddling. Add the advanced strokes later, as your skill and confidence in canoeing grow. Also keep in mind that canoeing conditions are so varied that no one stroke is ever perfect. Learn what works for you, and use that.

Practice your canoe strokes on a protected reach of flatwater, learning which strokes turn the canoe, and which direction the canoe turns. Also practice paddle teamwork in unison. Generally, bow paddlers set the paddling pace, because they can't look behind to watch the stern. The bow partner also watches for obstacles, especially in moving water, because the stern's view is obstructed. Much of the power in tandem paddling comes from the bow paddler, because the stern must deal with corrective strokes. The stern's job is keeping the canoe on course, and usually deciding where to go, after consulting with the bow. The stern can also assist with turning the canoe, besides making sure it stays on a straight line when canoeing from Point A to Point B.

And don't just paddle straight ahead. Go in circles, paddle backward, even sideways. Get comfortable with how your canoe handles with the different strokes.

To start the forward or power stroke (the basic canoeing stroke), rotate the body to plant the paddle blade in the water.

FORWARD OR "POWER" STROKE

Mastering this paddle stroke is 90 percent of canoeing, and quite easy. The forward stroke isn't just arm strength—use all of your upper body, so that paddling is more efficient and less tiring. The large muscles—shoulders, back, abdomen—are stronger than the arms. Let them work for you with this stroke.

In the forward stroke, the lower hand acts as a fulcrum, while the upper hand delivers power, which propels the canoe ahead. Because a canoeist might paddle as many as fourteen thousand strokes over a day, efficient form is crucial.

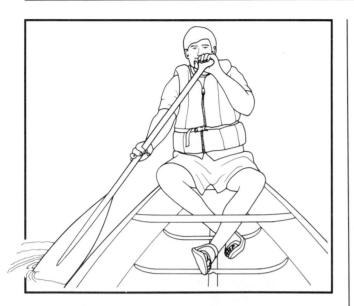

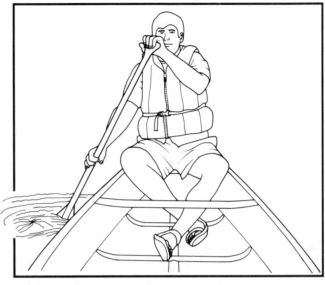

Plant the paddle blade in the water, then pull the paddle toward you. Note the difference between when the paddle shaft is vertical and when it is slightly angled. For best power, keep the paddle straight up and down.

Continue to pull the paddle toward yourself.

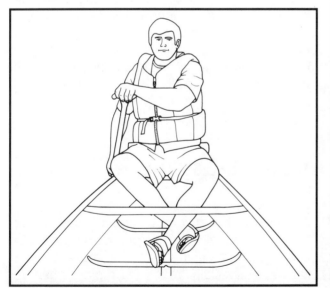

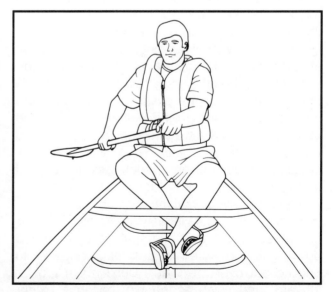

Stop the forward stroke at the hip and begin the recovery stroke.

Lift the paddle up out of the water and flatten out the blade.

Besides the official technique, consider also how your body reacts, as each person is a little different. For example, many canoeists paddle forward by raising the power arm high above the shoulders. Yet, for others, this will be tiring over the long haul. If paddling seems difficult, your stroke technique is probably to blame.

Start the forward stroke by gripping the paddle properly. Hold the grip with one hand, and grasp the paddle shaft near the throat with your other hand. The hands should be about shoulder width apart. Remember that the grip is controlled by the hand on the opposite side from where you are paddling. For example, if you're paddling on the left side, then the right hand controls the grip, while the left holds the shaft. Not holding the grip is a common mistake that greatly weakens paddling efficiency. Also, try to avoid plunging the lower hand into the water. There's no reason to get the lower hand wet, and wet hands are more prone to blistering.

To begin the forward stroke, use a 90-degree rotation of the upper body to plant the paddle into the water in front of you, reaching as far forward as you can without lunging, at least two feet ahead of you. Your top arm is bent and your bottom arm is straight. The top, or grip, supplies most of the power by pushing, while the lower hand guides during pulling. Submerge the blade of the paddle in the water, keeping it as close to the canoe as possible. Then pull with arm straight, keeping the paddle shaft vertical throughout the stroke. Now your top arm is straight, while your bottom arm is bent.

A common mistake is reaching across the body to stroke. Keep hands and shaft straight up and down over the water for best efficiency—avoid angling out over the water. Don't reach too far forward, and finish at the hip, because longer strokes waste energy. Also, don't let the upper arm drop down to the gunwale. Another mistake

is following the gunwale. Paddle in a straight line.

The forward stroke's recovery is more commonly referred to as "feathering" the paddle. Once the paddle blade has reached your hip, start the feathering by rotating the wrist of your top hand downward. This rotates the shaft in the lower hand, turning the paddle blade parallel (flat) to the water. Twist your trunk and shoulders to move the blade back "up" to the starting position. Now rotate your wrist and grip upward so that the blade's edge is in position for the next stroke.

Feathering the blade is done for several reasons. Most important, feathering cuts down on wind resistance by presenting a low profile to the wind during the recovery stroke. Feathering also gives your paddle strokes a smooth, elegant appearance. And, by using more muscles, feathering trains your body to be stronger. Many paddlers find that feathering the blade makes their wrists sore—at first. Once the wrist muscles adapt to the motion, and the forearms adjust to the new activity, your arms will grow stronger, better able to paddle longer with more efficiency. The forward paddle stroke combined with a feathering recovery stroke is excellent for building upper-body strength and endurance, while the feathering is especially good for wrist strength and flexibility.

THE REVERSE STROKE

This stroke is just the opposite of forward paddling. Backpaddling is useful for slowing the canoe, or even stopping it dead in the water. This is useful especially in running rapids, when you want to slow the canoe down to check out what's coming, and to resist the grabbing effect of a moving current.

REVERSE STROKE

To start the reverse stroke, plant the paddle in the water behind you.

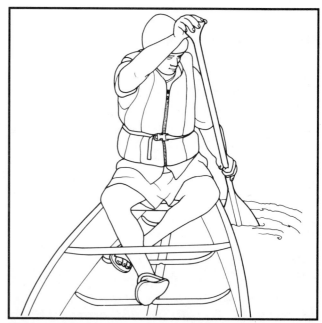

Push paddle forward, causing canoe to slow down in current or back up on flatwater.

Stop the reverse stroke before the paddle goes too far forward; going farther only wastes energy.

Rotate the blade so it is flat in the reverse stroke recovery. Return the paddle to your hip and take a second reverse stroke. (Reverse stroke recovery is the same as forward stroke, only in reverse.)

In the reverse stroke, the opposite side of the blade supplies the power. You use the same movements as the forward, only in reverse. Start with the shaft at the hip and the blade behind you, then push the blade forward, using the body to push the blade until the lower arm is fully extended. Recover by reversing the feathering stroke. How quickly the canoe slows down depends on how much force is used.

CORRECTIVE STROKES

Because canoeists must paddle a foot or more away from the keel line, the canoe doesn't track, or go straight, from just paddling forward or backward. Instead, the canoe veers away from the paddled side. To correct this trait, paddlers must employ corrective strokes like the J-stroke (below). Some canoeists maintain that switching sides often is more efficient than employing corrective strokes, but this can get tiring. A lot depends on what conditions you're paddling in. On flatwater, corrective strokes do impede forward momentum to a degree; in moving water, this isn't as noticeable. But in current, you're not working as hard to move the canoe forward.

In the tandem canoe, the paddler who sits in the stern is usually responsible for corrective strokes, because turning the canoe is easier from the stern. In a solo canoe, the paddler can employ corrective strokes from amidships, or switch sides, whichever is preferable.

THE J-STROKE

This stroke combines a forward motion with a corrective stroke, allowing the stern or solo paddler to easily keep the canoe going straight. Begin a forward stroke as usual. When the paddle reaches the hip and end of forward stroke, the thumb of the grip hand rotates down and away in a prying action, turning the power face of the blade outward. Be sure your thumb is pointed down, or you're doing the less-efficient stern pry stroke. Solo canoeists prefer the J-stroke to keep their craft tracking straight.

The J-stroke can be exaggerated to turn the canoe. The degree of turning depends on the degree of prying employed. Indeed, there are about

J-STROKE

Steps in the corrective J-stroke, done from stern or amidships in solo canoe, not bow. Start with a forward stroke . . .

as many variations on the basic J-stroke as there are canoeists.

Another option is using the paddle blade as a rudder, often with the shaft against gunwale or hip for additional leverage. This is an easy alternative—just hold the paddle behind you so that the blade rudders through the water. Ruddering slows forward momentum but offers a quick and simple method for tracking or turning. By leaning on the paddle as it rudders, you make the canoe pivot quickly. This corrective stroke is great for turning in rapids, when slowing down isn't a problem, and where the blade can catch current to affect the canoe's course.

When paddle reaches your hip, begin the outward curve of the J . . .

Use the top hand to rotate the blade outward in the J.

Paddle blade outward to finish J, then feather blade and return to forward stroke.

THE DRAW STROKE

Both draw and pry strokes are useful to move a canoe sideways in the water. They are similar strokes, like forward and reverse paddling. The draw stroke is used to move the canoe *toward* the side stroked. For instance, if you want the canoe to move left, then execute a draw stroke on the left side. To move right, stroke on the right side. This stroke can be accomplished in either bow or stern, or amidships for a solo paddler. The bow draw is often employed to move the bow sideways away from an approaching obstacle. The stern draw is used less often, but both paddlers in a tandem canoe should learn the draw; it comes in handy later for advanced maneuvers. Drawing is essential for eddy turns and other whitewater maneuvers, so if you aspire to paddle rapids, master this stroke.

To start the draw, reach with your body out over gunwale, extending the lower arm, with the upper arm bent. Plant the paddle blade directly out from your hip, with your chest facing the paddle. Now pull, or draw, the canoe toward the paddle. Stop before the blade reaches the canoe. For maximum power, you should be kneeling or well braced while drawing. The water's force has a counterbalancing effect on the canoe, so you can lean well out while drawing, to apply power with your entire body.

THE DRAW STROKE

Starting the draw stroke. Place blade out flat, then pull in toward you.

Draw stroke draws canoe toward paddle.

Continue.

Stop draw when blade is almost touching canoe. You are now ready for in-water recovery stroke.

Rotate blade so it is sideways. Blade should be submerged for most power (shown partially out of water here for illustration).

The recovery stroke is done under water, so it's a bit tricky. Rotate the paddle 90 degrees, turning the thumb of the grip, or top, hand away from you. This rotates the blade sideways. The blade's power face must be sideways so it slices through the water during recovery. If a second draw is necessary, the recovery stroke has left you in position to do another stroke, or you can switch back to forward paddling.

RECOVERY STROKE

Slice blade outward during in-water recovery stroke.

Keep blade sideways until starting position of draw is reached.

Rotate blade flat, power face toward canoe, for next draw.

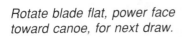

THE PRY STROKE

The pry stroke moves the canoe *away from* the side being stroked. Like the draw, the pry can be used from any position in the canoe. To start the pry, place the paddle blade under the canoe, then fully extend grip arm over water. Pull the grip across your chest as you push water away from the boat with your blade.

Some paddlers like to use a canoe's gunwale as a fulcrum point while doing a pry stroke. Hold the paddle shaft against the gunwale with your nongrip (lower) hand, then pry the blade outward.

This method isn't recommended for weak paddles, as the force can break them, or for moving water, because if the blade hits a rock, you can hurt your thumb.

As with the draw, paddle recovery is also under water. Turn the blade so that the top thumb is pointed outward, then slice the blade back under the canoe, never removing it from the water.

Many canoeists prefer to use the draw plus advanced strokes like the cross-bow and sweep to turn the boat, rather than the pry, believing that the pry slows momentum. Still, it's a useful counterpart to the draw, and easy to do.

PRY STROKE

Begin with blade flat against canoe. You can hold the shaft against gunwale with hand for greater fulcrum effect.

Pry blade outward, away from canoe.

Recovery stroke from pry is in-water. Rotate blade sideways, slice through water back to canoe.

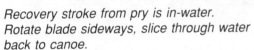

End of pry recovery stroke. Ready to start next pry.

THE SIDESLIP

Sideslipping simply means moving the entire canoe sideways. This maneuver is useful in whitewater to avoid broadsiding, so it's worth practicing in flatwater. To move the canoe sideways, a solo canoeist draws hard on one side, the side in the direction he or she wishes to move the canoe. In the tandem canoe, the two paddlers draw and pry simultaneously. Remember that you draw-stroke in the direction you wish to move, pry-stroke on the opposite side.

THE "HUT" STROKE—AND SWITCHING SIDES

In canoe racing, the word "hut" is the command for changing paddling sides simultaneously. While coordinating your paddling side changes isn't absolutely necessary, to maintain forward momentum, both paddlers should change sides at the same time. The advantage of yelling "Hut!" as both paddlers change sides is mostly fun, with a dab of convenience thrown in. Even if you aren't into racing, the hut stroke adds a bit of spice to paddling long, flat reaches. And kids love this maneuver.

To switch sides efficiently in the hut maneuver requires some coordination. Each paddler rotates the paddle to the opposite side by switching upper and lower hands simultaneously, in effect throwing the paddle from one side to the other and catching it in paddling position. Changing sides in this manner helps maintain the canoe's straightforward course. In addition, learning the hut stroke provides good practice for advanced strokes like the cross-bow draw. With or without

The sideslip. Both tandem partners need to work in unison to move the canoe sideways.

the hut stroke, changing sides at regular intervals lets one set of muscles rest while another set takes the brunt of the workout.

There is a clique of paddlers who feel that constantly changing sides while paddling—say about every six strokes or so—is more efficient for keeping the canoe on course than corrective strokes like the J-stroke. Others consider constant switching of sides a shining example of poor technique. Undoubtedly, switching sides keeps the canoe powering ahead, useful for plowing through whitecaps on a windy lake or getting to camp before dark. Indian tribes often used the hut stroke to great advantage, as do some solo paddlers today. (This technique of changing sides quickly and often is also known as the "Minnesota switch" from its use by canoe racers in that state.)

Release top hand as you begin
the switch.

Swing the paddle around.
Some canoeists like to keep
hands on the paddle and slide
the shaft to change sides,
others prefer this "toss and
catch" method.

Grasp throat of paddle
with both hands.

Rotate blade over to opposite
side as you reach for
grip with the top hand.

Keep the paddle moving while
your new grip hand
finds its mark.

At the end of the hut stroke, the
paddler is now set up on the
opposite side and is ready to
forward stroke.

CHAPTER 5

FLATWATER CRUISING

Beginners tend to think of all flatwater as easy water for canoeing. However, that placid lake you entered at mid-morning could have six-foot waves kicked up by wind gusts in late afternoon. Storms can blow in at any time, wreaking havoc for paddlers. Start with small ponds and sheltered coves for your first trips, to gain experience, skill, and confidence. Then move on to the bigger stuff.

LOADING THE CANOE

As with loading people, when loading gear for a day trip or camping expedition, load the canoe while it's floating in the water. Tossing a heavy ice chest into a beached canoe and then shoving the canoe into the water can cause damage, even with a tough boat. The best way to load is to pull the canoe sideways to the bank, then carefully lift items and set them down into the canoe.

Watch the trim of the canoe. Most canoes handle better when both ends are level. Keep weight close to center and as low as possible in the canoe. Use Duluth packs or dry bags for heavy gear—these are designed to fit low in the canoe.

KIDS IN CANOES

Start kids on easy water until they're used to canoeing. When canoeing with children, you'll want to have them sitting on the bottom until they learn to balance on the seats. Don't let anyone sit on the thwarts, regardless of what they weigh.

Thwarts are only to help maintain a canoe's stability and shape—they're not sturdy enough to be used as seats. Use only the floor or seats. Kids can even nap on the canoe floor. Provide padding (air mattress, closed-cell foam pads) and covers (perhaps a favorite fuzzy blanket for a younger child) so they'll have a cozy nest. Pads can double as backrests, to let kids sit back and look around, as well as insulation for sleeping.

Caution your kids about sudden movement in a canoe. They'll soon become accustomed to the way a canoe balances, because kids naturally have a lower center of gravity than adults. Even so, they should always wear properly fitting life jackets, just in case. More than just floating an overboard kid, PFDs keep the body core warm, which is important for anyone immersed in cold water.

Start kids out with short trips, depending on their ages. Younger children are apt to grow bored with being in a canoe all day. Let kids paddle, at least until they're tired, to keep them occupied and feeling like an important part of the whole adventure. Take breaks often to let everyone stretch their legs on a nature hike. Be sure to have plenty of energy-boosting snacks available for kids (jerky, fresh or dried fruits, nuts, fig bars, etc.) as well as lots of liquids (kids tend to dehydrate more quickly, even in cooler weather, so tempt them with fruit juices or milk from a Thermos if they fuss about water).

Keeping kids protected against cold, wet, and wind is particularly important. Beyond having to deal with a cranky child, remember that their small bodies lose heat faster. If they sit on the floor of the canoe, provide float cushions or similar elevated padding so they don't have wet seats. Dress them in good raingear and warm clothing. Raingear is important, but can be expensive with kids who outgrow everything. Good substitutions for smaller kids are ponchos, heavy-duty plastic "lawn and leaf" bags (with holes cut for arms and head, plus a hat), or a tarp to put over them. Always bring along a complete change of clothing. And don't overlook the problems created by heat. Protect against sunburn, glare, and chapped lips. In really hot conditions with small children, rig a tarp for shade in the canoe. Supervised swimming alongside the canoe is wonderful fun, besides a quick cool-off.

With all kids younger than teenage, be prepared to spend plenty of time wading in shallows after tadpoles, examining rocks and pine cones, chasing butterflies in the meadows, and other general messing around. This is perfectly normal, and the part of the trip your kids will always remember long after the memories of spectacular sunsets and scenic vistas have faded: time spent with the family. Canoeing with kids fosters warmth and togetherness, so why not start a new family tradition?

DEALING WITH WIND AND WAVES

Wind probably poses more problems for canoeists than any other force. Solo canoes in particular can be difficult to handle under windy conditions. Whenever the wind is blowing, it always seems as though it's deliberately trying to blow you in the wrong direction. There are several ways to deal with wind when canoeing. One way is to simply avoid it. Wind builds up as the day progresses—and is usually worse during the afternoon—so you can paddle very early in the morning, or late in the evening, when the wind doesn't blow. Paddling across a quiet lake in the moonlight is a special experience. Or, start your trip paddling upwind while you are fresh, so you don't have to fight it on the way back when you're tired.

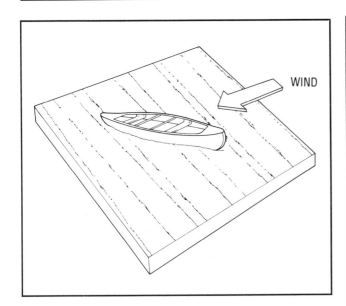

Quartering into wind and waves.

More likely, you will have to learn how to deal with wind for the majority of your canoeing hours. The best solution is to use the wind, to work with the gusts instead of struggling against them. You can lean the canoe away from the wind, so the wind glances off the bottom of the canoe. Then turn the canoe a few degrees off the wind. Now the wind will actually help propel the canoe.

A technique known as *quartering* is similar. Both methods allow the canoe to tack into the wind, much like a sailboat. To quarter, position the canoe to take wind at an angle. This moves the canoe forward in a straight line. Quartering also works with the waves kicked up by a strong wind. Instead of plowing straight through waves, take them at a 30- to 45-degree angle. This exposes more of the canoe's hull to the waves, makes a larger surface to resist splashes, and gives the bow more lift.

The further from shore you paddle, the bigger the waves. Paddling across the middle of a big, windy lake or reservoir can lead to disaster. Instead, try to hug the lee (wind sheltered) shoreline during gusty conditions. Shorelines always offer the safest routes on big lakes, because of wind-generated whitecaps. Avoid paddling across open stretches of water unless the day is very calm (and even then, conditions can change long before you reach the other side). Along shore, watch for waves kicked up by rivers entering the lake.

When faced with big waves on a lake, keep your wits about you. Lighten the ends so the canoe rides higher—paddlers may need to shift their weight forward of the stern and back from the bow. This helps shed spray from incoming waves, though some maneuverability is sacrificed. Lower your center of gravity by kneeling, or sit on the bottom of the canoe. Most important in heavy water, maintain your forward momentum by paddling hard. Dig paddles in to make headway during lulls. If conditions worsen, try to get to shore and wait for better weather. Especially dangerous is canoeing during a thunderstorm. Get to shelter!

Another technique for dealing with wind is using a sea anchor. This can be nothing more than a large (three- to five-gallon) bucket with an attached bail, or an elaborate parachutelike device often sold to sea kayakers. Tie the sea anchor to a long rope and throw it overboard. The open bucket or chute grabs water, stabilizing the canoe against the wind.

Going overboard in a windy situation can lead to disaster. Strong gusts can easily blow the canoe away from you, further than you can swim before exhaustion overtakes you. Should your canoe become swamped or overturned, stay with it (the canoe should still float) and try to empty the water, then reboard. Travel in groups of at least three canoes when crossing open waterways. If you must cross in a solo canoe, or undertake a risky crossing with just two canoes, consider rigging clip lines. These are short ropes with one end attached to the canoe, the other clipped to your body. Should you fall overboard, the clip line prevents the canoe from floating away. Clip lines are okay for use on deep lakes or on the ocean, but never use them on rivers, due to the risk of entanglement. A solo paddler would be wise to attach the paddle with a line as well.

DEALING WITH WAKES

Similar to wind-generated waves on a lake are the waves kicked up by passing motorcraft, known as *wakes.* Every motorized boat leaves a wake. The size of a wake depends on both the size of the boat and its speed. Wakes can rise up unexpectedly, surprising novice canoeists and overturning their canoes.

To ride out a wake, turn the canoe so that the bow is pointing directly into the rolling waves of the wake. Paddle hard into the waves to keep the canoe straight. If you know how to brace, now is the time to try out that skill. With a big wake, you might need to quarter into the waves; otherwise the canoe could swamp.

Whenever paddling in areas frequented by motorized craft, canoeists should be alert for wakes, besides making sure that the boat operator has spotted them and is giving them room. A canoe has the right of way over a powered craft, but don't expect all motorized boats to yield. Most canoeists prefer to avoid waterways heavily traveled by motorized craft due to the "jerk factor" seemingly always present in a small percentage of motorboat jockeys. Thousands of waterways

accessible only to canoes beckon; why choose a crowded area?

WATER IN THE CANOE

Even under the best of conditions, a canoe can take on water. The low sides and narrow shape of a canoe allow waves to enter. Small amounts of water present no special problems—your bailer and sponge are all you need. Be sure to attach a short line with a clip, or a rock climber's carabiner, to the bailer so it won't be lost overboard when not in use.

If your canoe should become swamped—filled with water—take action immediately to avert a dangerous situation. A swamped canoe is extremely heavy, particularly if a strong current is pushing on it. The waterlogged canoe will also be difficult to maneuver. On flatwater, stay with an overturned or swamped canoe because the canoe won't sink and still provides good flotation. But the canoe can be damaged while wallowing around, especially in shallows, so you'll want to empty the water out as soon as possible.

Water can be emptied from the canoe with the assistance of another boat, by tipping it over, if you're able to, or sometimes by holding one end and giving the canoe a vigorous shake, called a *shakeout.* The shakeout should be used only in deep water.

If the canoe is overturned, righting it is easiest with another canoe. Use the canoe-over-canoe rescue: The assisting canoeists grab the overturned canoe, hoist it across the middle of their canoe, then right the canoe and place it back in the water. If there are no helping hands, you'll need to right the canoe yourself by pulling on the gunwales. Or you can rig a line across the middle of the canoe as a righting aid. Some canoeists prefer to swim the canoe to shore, using the painter, but in deep water, this option may be impossible.

To get back in safely, grasp the far gunwale and pull yourself up on the near gunwale, balancing your body flat over the canoe. Then gradually climb in, keeping your weight over the keel line. An overboard person should be brought in much the same way so he or she doesn't upset the canoe while scrambling to get back in.

HYPOTHERMIA

If the water is cold and paddlers have gone overboard—or have gotten soaked by waves and are now being blown by wind—consider the situation an emergency. Get the canoeing party to shore and begin hypothermia treatment. If you're on the middle of a large lake, you will have to unpack dry clothes and warm blankets on the spot. In such a situation, you must work fast to prevent the dangerous lowering of body temperature caused by cold water combined with wind (and possibly fatigue) known as *hypothermia*. This—not raging whitewater or unseen waterfalls—is the greatest risk of canoeing.

Preferable to treatment is remaining aware of hypothermia so that this life-threatening condition may be prevented. Averting the onset of hypothermia is much easier than stopping its course. Start with proper clothing to protect against wind and wet. Life jackets are especially important, because they cover the central body core and vital organs, trapping heat inside their thick foam flotation. Follow up with high-calorie food and hot drinks (brewed on land, or use a Thermos) to keep the body stoked with fuel. Hard paddling de-

lays shivering, as does any vigorous exercise, but also drains the body. Paddlers should keep a watchful eye on each other, because a classic symptom of hypothermia is denial. At the first sign of chills, head for shore and shelter. In the early stages of hypothermia, your body still possesses the ability to rewarm itself, but as the condition progresses, external sources of heat must be used. Uncontrollable shivering, generally, is the first sign that this border has been crossed. Treat a shivering victim seriously. Other symptoms are a loss of judgment and coordination.

In a real emergency, drastic measures must be used to prevent loss of life. Before the victim slips too far away, use external sources of heat to rewarm as fast as possible. This may mean building a big fire, wrapping the victim in warm clothes and sleeping bags, deploying chemical-fired heat packs around the torso, or, if nothing else is available, skin-to-skin rewarming. Never give alcohol—it dilates the blood vessels, increasing heat loss, despite a temporary feeling of warmth.

If you become submerged in water without immediate rescue, your options are more limited. First, always try to get out of the water and onto a boat, even an overturned canoe. A solo swimmer can assume a fetal position that conserves body heat. Several paddlers should huddle together. If no other boats or rescue are in sight, such as on a wilderness lake, seriously consider swimming to shore. This will drain vital body heat faster, plus contribute to exhaustion, yet in cold water, self-rescue may be your only viable option. Better still is avoiding this situation with clip lines, so you at least have your canoe close by.

EXPANDING YOUR CANOEING ENJOYMENT

After some time spent learning to use your canoe, you will be ready to expand your canoeing enjoyment. You've already seen that the canoe can be paddled on flatwater and whitewater, out for an afternoon or on expeditions, in pleasant summer conditions or during cold weather. With a few basic additions, your canoe can become another boat entirely, increasing the range of activities. Some worthwhile accessories that are nice to have (yet not essential for starting out) are sail kits, rowing setups, motor and mount, or pontoons for stability.

SAILING A CANOE

When the wind is blowing right, it's fun to hoist a makeshift sail—a tarp tethered between two paddles, for instance—and let nature move the canoe. With two canoes, you can even create a sort of catamaran by hitching them together with two long poles. Send up a sail, and the canoes will fly across the water.

Beyond such improvisations, most any canoe can be easily converted into a serious sailboat with the addition of a sailing kit. For real sailing, you'll need a sail, a way to control the canoe (leeboards, rudder), a mast and mast support, plus rigging (cleats to hold the ropes used in raising and lowering the sail). Several canoe companies sell sailing conversion kits, or an inventive sailor can construct his or her own by assembling the various components.

If you're interested in sailing your canoe, check out how-to-sail lessons offered at most locations where wind and water meet. Even boardsailing provides the basic knowledge necessary for understanding how wind propels a boat. But serious sailing without lessons is difficult.

Properly equipped, canoes make delightful small sailboats. They're responsive and fun, without the hassles connected to bigger boats, like trying to find dock space, a rare commodity in most harbors, or licensing. Canoe conversions offer a relatively inexpensive, easily accessible introduction to sailing.

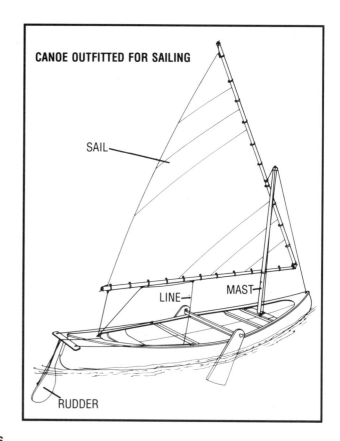

CANOE OUTFITTED FOR SAILING

SAIL

LINE

MAST

RUDDER

ROWING A CANOE

As the popularity of rowing shells soars, converting your canoe into a rowboat beckons. Why purchase another boat when the canoe can do the job nearly as well, and for much less money? As with sailing kits, you can purchase rowing kits for many breeds of canoes, or inventive canoeists can devise their own. Especially nice are sliding seat arrangements that exercise all major muscle groups. Sculling your canoe across a lake is great exercise that also soothes the nerves. A canoe rigged for rowing has more maneuverability than a traditional rowboat, plus some of a racing shell's speed. The combination can be an exhilarating alternative to paddling.

Besides oars, you'll need some kind of seat (sliding, for greater leg exercise, or stationary, more stable in the canoe), plus a framework to support the oars (oarlocks and oar stands). Oar collars keep the oars from sliding out of open oarlocks (the kind that look like the letter *U*), while pin-and-clip arrangements keep the oars attached to the oar stands with the blades held in vertical position (necessary for proper rowing). Another device, called "Oar Rights," maintains the vertical position of oar blades in open oarlocks.

PONTOONS

Adding pontoons—a pair of buoyant tubes that straddle both sides of a canoe amidships—greatly increases stability. Some like these floats when paddling with children or disabled individuals, simply for the added peace of mind. Pontoons are useful, too, for braving big water in the middle of a lake. You can buy pontoons from some canoe suppliers, or rig your own. If you've always dreamed of boating in the South Pacific, you can even use the pontoons to create an outrigger canoe (usually one float instead of two).

MOTORING A CANOE

Yes, we're canoeing in the first place to avoid motors, because of all the noise, smell, and hassles they generate. Yet motors do have their place in canoeing. For example, if you want to go upriver against even the most moderate current, paddling is next to impossible, but a motor can manage, allowing round-trip canoeing from one launch site.

And certainly crossing a big reservoir loaded with powerboats is easier if you also have a motor. Motors are also useful when drifting downstream, to motor through flats and speed up the trip. Fishermen sometimes like to use a small motor on their canoes for trolling, or to hold against the current in a spot where the fish are biting.

Whatever your reasoning, if you wish to attach a motor to your canoe, first you'll have to consider licensing requirements in your area for motorized craft. Then comes the problem of attaching the motor. A square-stern canoe is ideal—this design was created with motorization in mind. Or you can acquire a side-mounting bracket for your canoe motor.

A canoe motor must be modest, usually limited to three horsepower, or it will overwhelm the canoe. An electric trolling motor that runs off battery power works well—no smell and less noise. How-

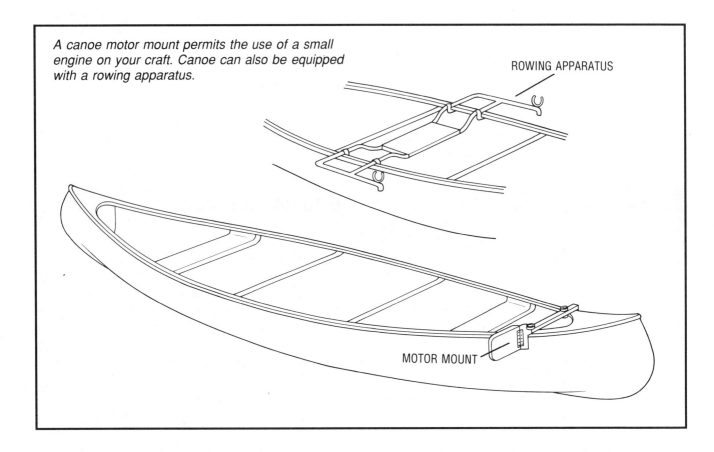

A canoe motor mount permits the use of a small engine on your craft. Canoe can also be equipped with a rowing apparatus.

ROWING APPARATUS

MOTOR MOUNT

ever, range is limited. Gas-powered motors are more powerful and can go further for the same weight (gas in a can, as opposed to electricity stored in a battery). When motoring a canoe, carry extra fuel, a motor repair kit (with tools plus a square prop, as these are often broken in shallow water), paddles (in case of engine failure), and a fire extinguisher.

CHAPTER 6

ADVANCED CANOEING TECHNIQUES

SWEEP STROKES

Sweep strokes are simply exaggerations of the forward and backward strokes—executed as you "sweep" the paddle, broomlike, by reaching out further from the canoe. Because both forward and back sweeps allow turning without slowing momentum, sweeps are often preferred over other corrective strokes, especially the pry.

Sweep strokes may be executed from either bow or stern. Both partners in a tandem canoe should practice sweeps and become familiar with how the boat moves during sweep strokes, to make best use of their powerful motion. The greater the amount of rocker your canoe possesses, the more effective sweep strokes will be—they're great for turning in whitewater.

For a forward sweep, place your paddle far for-ward, then sweep outward in a wide arc. Stop when the paddle is even with your hip. Recover as in a regular forward stroke. The back sweep is just the reverse.

BRACE STROKES

In a brace stroke, the paddler leans out of the canoe, bracing his or her weight against the paddle to stabilize the canoe. The paddle acts as an outrigger or pontoon, making the canoe, in effect, wider and more stable. Essential in whitewater to prevent upsets, braces also come in handy for mastering big waves on a lake. Practice brace strokes first in a safe place, because the leaning necessary for bracing may result in overboards.

Both partners in a tandem canoe can utilize the sweep strokes for turning the canoe.

There are two kinds of brace strokes: high brace and low brace. Both somewhat resemble the draw stroke and involve sculling the blade. The high brace is accomplished at a 90-degree angle. Keep the upper hand high, above the head. Press down and draw toward the canoe. Slap the blade on the water surface, sculling back and forth, to maintain the lean.

In the low brace, the paddle is almost parallel to the water's surface. The palm of the grip hand should face upward. Lean out and put your weight on the paddle.

Braces are very stable when moving because the paddle planes on the water. You must keep the paddle at just the correct angle. If the blade goes too deep, you may follow it down.

Here is the high brace on a calm lake . . .

. . . and the same high brace in whitewater. Note that this paddler is bracing and leaning downstream.

THE SWEEP STROKE

Start the forward sweep by reaching forward, as in the regular forward stroke.

Now sweep the paddle outward in a wide arc.

Submerge the blade for most power in the sweep. (This canoeist is keeping the blade partway above water for demonstration purposes.)

Finish the forward sweep at the hip.

Recovery stroke after a sweep is feathered like a regular forward stroke.

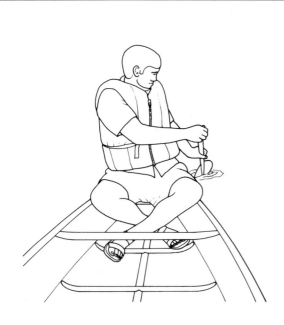

Start behind you at the hip as in a regular reverse.

Now push the paddle around in a wide arc.

Continue the sweep until the blade is alongside your body.

The recovery stroke begins here.

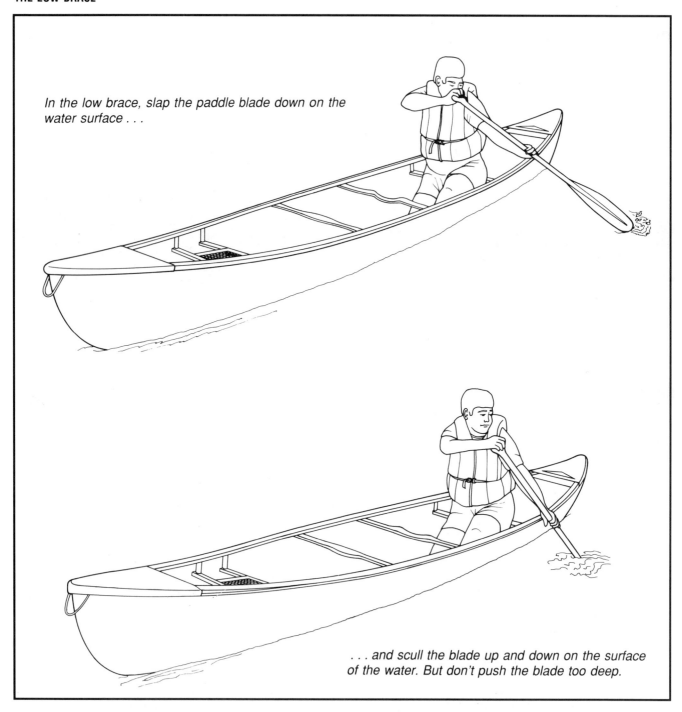

In the low brace, slap the paddle blade down on the water surface . . .

. . . and scull the blade up and down on the surface of the water. But don't push the blade too deep.

84

CROSS-BOW DRAW

This is a dramatic stroke, but also difficult for beginners to master. In the cross-bow draw, the canoe must be moving forward at a good clip—usually with a current. The stroke pivots the bow into the direction of the stroke. To cross-bow draw, reach across the bow of the canoe to the offside, then place the paddle blade in the water at a 10-degree angle. Draw stroke toward the bow. The fast turn results from the blade working as a rudder in the current, using the force of the water to pull the bow around. Perhaps the hardest part of the stroke is timing—knowing when to

CROSS-BOW RUDDER STROKE

To begin, get ready to change paddle sides in the bow.

Change sides quickly without altering your grip.

Plant the paddle blade into the water on the opposite side of the canoe without changing grip.

CROSS-BOW DRAW

The cross-bow draw is similar to the rudder stroke. Instead of planting the blade and holding it there, plant the blade . . .

. . . and draw the blade toward you as in a regular draw stroke.

stop paddling on the opposite side, shifting the paddle quickly, and drawing. Another option is to plant the blade in the current for the cross-bow rudder stroke.

THE CANADIAN STROKE

In this version of the J-stroke, the paddle stays in the water during the entire stroke. Start as though doing a J-stroke, then execute a partial water recovery. The additional steering action comes from pulling hard as the paddle blade is sliced forward through the recovery stroke. The Canadian stroke is considered more elegant than the J-stroke, as well as more efficient.

THE INDIAN STROKE

This stroke is simply a forward stroke with an in-water recovery, instead of feathering the blade. The name *Indian stroke* derives from its silence, useful for sneaking up on wildlife. Rotate the paddle grip in your hand so that as the blade enters recovery, it is on edge, slicing quietly though the water. This stroke is also useful for controlling the canoe under windy conditions.

SCULLING

Sculling is a variation on the draw stroke. When sculling, instead of pulling the paddle toward the canoe, you work the paddle blade back and forth in the water. Sculling provides a continuous brac-

ing effect as the paddle blade remains in the water. The action is much like an in-water recovery for a draw stroke except that the blade is kept parallel to the canoe, rather than knifed sideways.

PADDLING WITH DOUBLE BLADES

The traditional kayak paddle permits fast movement through slow water, in particular through weedy sloughs, as well as effective solo or adult/child canoeing. This paddle can be used with both blades flat (unfeathered), but most prefer to work with one blade set at a 90-degree angle to the other (feathered), highly effective against wind. Stroking with an unfeathered paddle requires no special skills—just paddle forward or backward on both sides alternately, or on one side for turning. Unfeathered blades really get the canoe moving when the wind is blowing from behind. Draw and pry strokes are clumsier, but not necessary if you utilize sweeps or reverse strokes for pivoting.

A feathered paddle is more complex. The easiest way to proceed is to designate one hand as the "power hand"—almost always the right. Remember that the paddle shaft rotates in the power hand only during recovery of the power-side blade. Grip firmly with the power hand, loosely with the other. After the power hand takes a stroke, the opposite blade isn't in proper position to stroke. The blade must be rotated into position by cocking or twisting the nonpower (left) wrist. This causes the shaft to rotate the blade into paddling position. When you finish the stroke, the power side will be out of position. Correct by cocking the power wrist downward while rotating the shaft in the nonpower hand. Now the power side is once again ready for action.

With the feathered blades, you don't have to worry about special recovery strokes, since the rotation of blades performs this chore for you. Not only does working the feathered blade sound difficult, but some paddlers find this wrist rotation clumsy at first . . . so plenty of practice is in order.

Using a double-bladed paddle takes a number of steps, but it appears more complicated than it is. This is a nine-foot paddle with feathered blades. Stroke forward on one side, then rotate the shaft so that the other blade is in the forward paddle position. The recovery strokes are accomplished automatically.

THE CANOE POLE

Poling a canoe is almost a lost art. Once a common way to work a canoe up slow or shallow streams, poling is now mostly a curiosity. As more people develop an interest in the heritage of canoeing, though, poling is gradually making a comeback. The basic idea is pretty simple. You use a long stick (wood or aluminum, twelve feet long), standing up in the canoe for the most part, and move the canoe by pushing down on the stick, working hand over hand. Commercial poles come with special tips that poke into a river bottom for better traction in mud and gravel. You can buy a "setting pole," or buy just the tip and make your own pole if you have access to saplings.

Most difficult is learning to balance yourself while standing in the canoe, especially for upstream movements against a current. Your weight distribution in the canoe is important. Often, instead of standing, you crouch for better balance. In the hands of an expert, poling is a surprisingly efficient method for propelling a canoe, upstream in particular. Even slowing and controlling the canoe's path downstream through tricky rapids and river currents (known as "snubbing") is possible, with sufficient experience. Learn paddle techniques first, then try poling. Chances are you'll get dunked a lot while practicing, but that's part of the challenge poling offers. Try late summer's warmer, slower, shallow flows for fun poling practice.

SOLO CANOE PADDLING

Sitting in the middle converts most any canoe into a solo canoe. With all the weight in the center, the ends are lighter, rising and falling in the waves. If you have a tandem canoe and want to sample soloing, try paddling without a partner to get a feel for the solo canoe. Most difficult in a makeshift solo canoe is tracking, especially when the wind is blowing. Without the stabilizing influence of a partner, the soloist often needs strong J-strokes to keep the canoe going straight. A "C" stroke—reaching out from the canoe, sweeping in and then out again (just like the letter C when paddling on the right side)—is also useful. Solo canoeists using tandems resort to hut stroking—switching sides often—or even the double-bladed paddle, for increased directional control.

Modern solo canoes are designed to track better with one paddler sitting amidships. An experienced paddler in a good hull design can make a solo canoe fly. Keep this in mind when soloing in a tandem. One way to paddle solo in a larger canoe is to pack gear around the bow seat, substituting its weight for the weight of the bow partner. Now the canoe won't try to veer away from your paddling side as much, because your stroke is closer to the keel line. In rough water, though, you'll want to be further forward.

LINING AND TRACKING PAST RAPIDS

Lining is leading a canoe downstream on a rope "leash" as one would lead a dog. *Tracking* usually refers to pulling the canoe upstream by a tethered rope. As a less-strenuous alternative to portaging the canoe, lining is worth considering whenever you are faced with unrunnable water.

The best way to line a canoe is to use two separate ropes. A canoe's painters will work if they're long enough. Two canoeists work together: One takes the downstream line, angling the boat around obstacles, while the second slows the rate of descent with the stern line, or brake.

Always wear a life jacket when lining a canoe, and make sure all gear is securely tied in. For control in very fast current, snub the stern line around a tree or rock onshore, then pay it out slowly. Use floating line so the rope won't sink and hang up underwater. Keep lines taut to avoid entanglement, and stay clear of the lines. Don't allow anyone to ride in the canoe being lined—it could flip over. Work slowly and carefully, as lining can be dangerous work if rushed.

In a modest current, the canoe can be lined with a single rope. All lining ropes are best secured low around the canoe, through holes or loops close to the waterline, or you can rig a harness around the bottom of the canoe and tie to the thwarts.

When lining, don't let the canoe get broadside to the current. Should the canoe be pulled sideways, snub the upstream line. If painters aren't long enough, use your rescue rope.

It is important when tracking upstream against a rapid to avoid heavy current; portage instead. Tracking uses angle to the current to propel the canoe. Alter the angle by pulling on the line, and the canoe returns to shore.

Neither lining nor tracking is feasible where shorelines are cluttered with debris or thick vegetation. But in open country, these techniques can save the trouble of unpacking and carrying gear in addition to portaging the canoe.

WADING A CANOE

Wading a canoe offers another alternative to portaging, when the conditions are right. Wading is great in warm weather, through shallow water without a lot of current. Be wary of wading in deep water. Work with a partner, holding the gunwales of the canoe for balance and security in a current, and watch out for each other. Always wear PFDs.

THE PORTAGE TRAIL

As you see, some paddlers will do just about anything to get out of portaging. But despite the popular conception of portaging a canoe as a Herculean task, carrying a canoe need not be such an arduous chore. Careful consideration of the situation can really take the sting out of portaging, so don't be so averse to carrying the canoe instead of paddling uncertain stretches. Never underestimate the power of whitewater: When in doubt, portage.

And don't let the thought of portages scare you away from a canoe trip. Portages are what make travel by canoe unique. After all, how many forms of transportation allow you to carry around an unnegotiable spot? Also, portages take you away from civilization. The more portages, and the harder they are, the fewer people. And the only folks you'll see out there are fellow canoeists—no motorboaters or water-skiers! On the portage trail, you stretch your legs, a welcome change of pace from paddling.

First, look for a portage trail. Most portages along popular routes will have a well-used trail, often marked by a sign or a tree blaze. Check your map as well. In remote areas, you will have to find your own route. Scout the trail first with light packs, so you are familiar with the path and won't get sidetracked. On a long trail, watch for a rest spot where you can set the end of the canoe down and walk out from underneath. The forked branch of a tree works well for this.

A good yoke—a padded thwart attached to the canoe, or a device that fits over the center thwart of the canoe, specifically for carrying—certainly makes portaging easier. The purpose of a yoke is to distribute weight evenly over your body. You can buy, make, or improvise a yoke on the spot. Some canoeists use a cheap horsecollar life jacket to pad their shoulders against the canoe's weight, others tie two paddles into the open canoe to serve as the yoke. Before a trip requiring several portages, or long carries, install a yoke (you can always remove it later). The yoke is most useful for carrying a canoe solo. If you have a partner to help carry, you may elect to carry the canoe low, so your vision isn't impaired. Or you may prefer to balance the canoe on your shoulders as you trek the trail. Choose the carrying option that works best for you.

Wilderness canoeists who portage a lot prefer wooden yokes to aluminum. Wood is warmer and more flexible than aluminum. For exact placement of the yoke, practice balancing the canoe on your shoulders until it feels right to you. The two pads of the yoke should rest squarely on your shoulders. Some canoeists like to rig a tumpline for long, hard carries of both canoe and packs. Early voyagers often carried up to 180 pounds per trip across tough portages by using this special forehead strap.

Gear on canoe trips with portages is packed into Duluth packs or other packs with shoulder straps so it can be easily toted down the portage trail. Otherwise, you have to gather up handfuls of things and carry them loose in your arms. Carrying things in the canoe is not a good idea, except for very small items.

CANOE REPAIRS

Before heading out on a whitewater trip or a wilderness expedition, be familiar with the methods recommended for repairing your particular type of canoe, and pack along an appropriate repair kit. If you are part of a group in which several different hull materials are represented, make sure that all the right repair items are taken along.

With an aluminum canoe, dents are the most common damage. In the field or at home, you can pound out, or stomp on, dents to minimize them. Liquid solder or epoxy can fix a hole, at least until you can get the canoe to an aluminum welding shop for a more permanent repair. Duct tape will reinforce these repairs, or cover tiny spots. This miracle material is useful for fixing other types of canoes, and for just about anything that breaks down in the field, like your paddles or tent. Use quality duct tape—fabric coated with plastic, not just plastic alone.

Fiberglass is the easiest to patch. You'll want to patch both inside and outside for a secure hull. Sand the area to be patched, apply resin, and sand again after it's cured. Be sure to select a resin that's compatible with the kind of fiberglass canoe you have. Kevlar is patched much the same way, but again, check with the canoe manufacturer before attempting repairs. Fiberglass patches are sometimes used on wood canoes, too.

CHAPTER 7

GETTING YOUR FEET WET IN WHITEWATER

In the past, canoeists intent on transporting furs and other trade goods cursed whitewater; rapids often meant long, hard portages. Today, rapids offer fun and excitement, as canoeists travel for pleasure rather than profit. Running rapids is safer now than ever before, with modern, improved equipment, plus better canoeing skills and techniques. Special whitewater canoes go right over rocks and plunge through waves with ease in the hands of an experienced paddler. Even the recreational canoeist can enjoy moderate whitewater in relative safety, if he or she understands and observes a few basic safety precautions.

River paddling uses the same paddling skills you've already learned on flatwater. Now you just need to learn how to apply them on moving water. Remember that the force exerted by moving water is deceptively powerful. Because the current is constantly moving, you must be alert, and keep the canoe under control at all times. Not only does a river present more canoeing obstacles, but the current takes you right into them unless you respond with the correct maneuvers. Rivers offer a real challenge for canoeists.

To counteract current, you dictate speed. Easiest is to drift with current—if the river is slow, this is efficient and enjoyable. The speed of the river depends on several factors, chiefly *gradient* (how much elevation loss over a particular stretch of riverbed, usually expressed in terms of feet per mile) and *volume* (how much water the river carries, usually expressed in cubic feet per second).

On a faster river, you can take a conservative route by slowing down against the current to maneuver or look something over. Or you can paddle faster than the current, to land in an eddy, punch through big waves, or maybe just savor the thrill of speed. Start out with a slow descent as

◄ Canoeing whitewater is an exhilarating experience—if you develop your river sense.

Once you learn how to paddle safely through whitewater, you're ready to tackle "playboating." This canoeist is "surfing" upstream in heavy hydraulics. He makes it look easy! ►

you learn how to handle whitewater, saving power strokes for climbing over waves and hydraulics. Paddling hard in whitewater is exciting, but it also drives the canoe faster toward obstacles.

REVIEWING A RIVER

Before you attempt canoeing on a local river, investigate. River trips are considered in terms of stretches, or what the river is like from one launch site to the next. Find out what conditions to expect on the particular stretch of river that you're interested in floating. What classification of white-

water will be encountered, and are your canoeing skills sufficient to handle it (or can you portage or line, if not)? What flow is considered ideal, and where do you find out the river's present water level? Many popular rivers have water levels given daily on a recorded "flow phone" you can call. Also worth investigating are special obstacles (new trees washed down by a recent flood, for instance), water temperature (will you wear shorts or rent a wet suit), distance between rapids (nonstop rapids don't allow recovery time, or mean a long portage) and any other factors contributing to the difficulty of the run. And consider, too, how many miles you'll be paddling between access points. A canoeist in current can paddle fifty miles in one day, but for an average outing, figure on ten to twenty miles.

An excellent choice for accurate information is a canoe livery along the stretch of river you plan to run, especially if you will be renting a canoe from them. Liveries will be frank with you because they don't want their canoes damaged. River rangers, too, are prime sources, as they don't want to rescue you! Guidebooks also offer good general information, but watch out for books emphasizing rafting or kayaking—these tend to underrate rapids that can be difficult for canoeists. Other canoeists, especially those in paddling clubs, can give you information about good places to go in your area, too.

Ask about a river's suitability for canoes and honestly describe your skill level, as well as what kind of canoe you'll be paddling, and how it's equipped (with or without spray covers, etc.). Also check with maps for access points, for launching, taking out, or for walking out if the river proves too much. Whenever consulting any publication, look for the current copyright date—older river descriptions could be out-of-date as rivers are constantly changing. Just before embarking, check the water levels again.

And never take a river for granted. Many canoeists are fooled by a long, deceptively calm stretch of river under a highway bridge at a boat launch site. That calm pool could turn into roaring rapids just around the first bend. Beware of easy-appearing flatwater at highway bridges and other accesses.

Inflatable canoes make excellent whitewater playboats. This inflatable canoe has blunt tips to avoid "diving" into hydraulics. Note upstream paddling position for "surfing" small reversal.

LEARNING TO READ A RIVER

The skill of discerning what lies ahead on a river seems mysterious, but in reality is easy to develop. Whether in Alaska or Africa, rivers share common characteristics that can be "read" just like a book. With experience, a good boater can recognize hazards far upstream and easily navigate around them.

When you sit in a canoe on a river, you are headed downstream. The region behind you is upstream. River runners always face downstream, looking ahead, so they can see what is coming. As you face downstream, the area to your left is referred to as "river left," while the right side is, you guessed it, "river right." Downstream is always the direction of the current.

Rocks are the most common obstacle encountered along rivers. Hitting a rock with your canoe, even a tough canoe, is best avoided. To recognize rocks, look for the "flag" signaling impeded water: V-shaped formations on the water's surface. An upstream V indicates a rock at the sharp tip of the V. On the other hand, a V pointing downstream shows gaps between rocks. The smooth water between two rocks often offers the best route for a canoe, and may be called a tongue, slot, slick, channel, or simply a V. As you study a rapid, look for other indications of impeded current that signal "rock": water shooting straight up (often referred to as a "rooster tail"), water humping up, or spray that doesn't come from a wave. Sometimes a hint of darkness can be glimpsed beneath the whitewater.

When rocks or other major obstacles block the river's flow, the current flows around, creating a calm pool below the obstacle. This haven in the middle of a rapid is called an *eddy*. Eddies also develop below shoreline outcroppings, behind logs—anywhere the current is impeded. Some-

"Strainers" have dangerous currents and should be avoided. Keep to the inside of river bends to avoid unpleasant surprises around sharp corners, and give logs a wide berth. (This particular strainer has been dubbed the "Death Log" because a paddler was sucked under and nearly killed.)

times this backwash flows upriver. Eddies are important to canoeists because they slow or stop the canoe, along the shore or even right in the middle of a rapid. Where the eddy meets the flowing current, there's an abrupt change of current known as the eddy line or fence. Crossing this line can be tricky for canoes, sometimes resulting in an upset if the paddlers aren't prepared to handle the strong currents. The end of an eddy is called an *eddy tail*. Learn to recognize eddies; in big rapids, they're a canoeist's best friend. Once you can spot an eddy, the next step is to master the eddy turn, landing your canoe in the eddy.

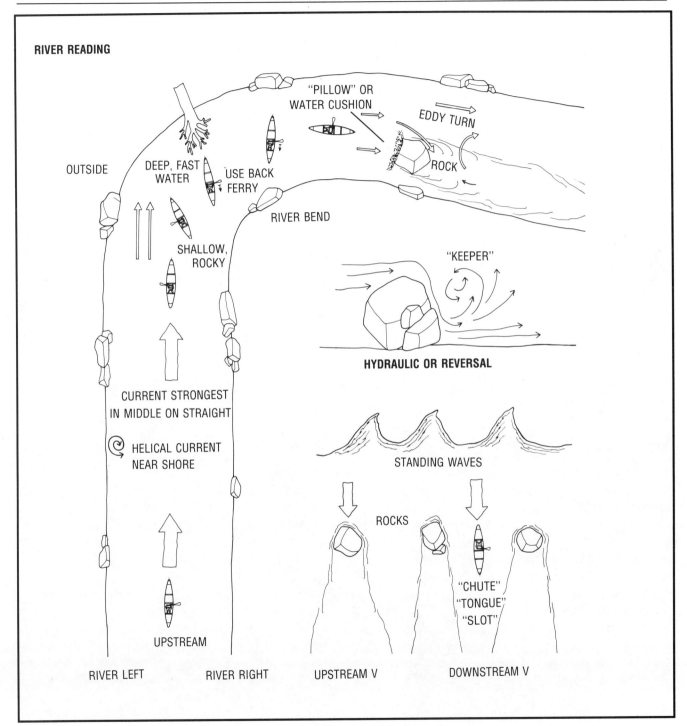

RIVER READING

"PILLOW" OR WATER CUSHION

EDDY TURN

OUTSIDE

DEEP, FAST WATER

USE BACK FERRY

ROCK

RIVER BEND

SHALLOW, ROCKY

"KEEPER"

HYDRAULIC OR REVERSAL

CURRENT STRONGEST IN MIDDLE ON STRAIGHT

HELICAL CURRENT NEAR SHORE

STANDING WAVES

ROCKS

"CHUTE"
"TONGUE"
"SLOT"

UPSTREAM

RIVER LEFT

RIVER RIGHT

UPSTREAM V

DOWNSTREAM V

Outside of a protected eddy, the current along a river shore is not necessarily calm. Instead, spiraling currents known as *helical currents* are often encountered, especially on faster streams. These tend to push a boat or swimmer away from shore. For this reason, landing a canoe, or swimming to shore along a river with moderate speed can be difficult. Again, you need to recognize eddy water and take advantage of the upstream currents to safely land your canoe.

Rushing water follows the course of least resistance. By looking at a river, you can predict where the current is fastest: midstream, where the flow encounters less resistance. On the inside of a bend, the current will be slower, the riverbed

This canoeist in the stern is using thigh straps. The pair of tandem canoeists sit closer together to let canoe ends lift and leave more room for flotation.

shallower. Because the current slows, sand and gravel build up on the inside banks. Water around the outside of a bend picks up more speed. Because of this speed, gravel doesn't get deposited very deep—it washes right through—so the outside of a bend offers deeper water than the inside. Obstacles such as trees fallen into the river also are more prevalent on the outside of bends, as the faster current sweeps into the banks, eroding roots and pushing debris into the water.

A smart canoeist, understanding this, keeps to the inside of a blind corner—just far enough inside to avoid the faster current and its obstacles, without getting into the shallows found far inside. This is known as "cheating" or "sneaking" the route, an intelligent procedure if you don't know what's coming up around the bend. Unless you land the canoe and walk ahead to look ("scouting" a rapid), plan on keeping to the inside of a river bend.

Those overhanging branches and trees collapsing into the river present a major hazard to river floating. Canoeists call them strainers, sweepers, or alligators, depending on whether they strain the current, sweep downriver, or pop up unexpectedly in front of the canoe. By any name, they're dangerous and should be given a wide berth. Branches in the current let water run through, but trap anything else that tries to go through, including canoes and paddlers.

If you ever do find yourself headed straight for a downed tree, as a last resort, try to reach up and grab on to a branch, then pull yourself up, so you don't get sucked underneath. Otherwise, never latch on to overhanging branches. Some novice canoeists can't resist the temptation, and usually wind up yanked right out of their canoes. Avoid all vegetation along a waterway whenever possible. If you must float under a branch, duck forward and not to the side, to maintain balance.

Another predictable feature of rivers is the divided channel. A river may split around a large obstacle, usually an island, then rejoin further downstream. This poses a puzzle: which branch to follow? The best choice is a major channel that is well known. Minor channels may dead-end or surprise you with a dangerous logjam. Previous knowledge of the river is the favored way to select which channel to take.

Lacking this, you may have to get out of the canoe and scout for a safe channel. Look for the signs of a major channel: the fork that drops first and carries more water. If in doubt, always take a channel that offers a clear passage, rather than a blind corner.

Recognizing different types of rivers offers a shortcut to understanding them. Many rivers are described as "pool and drop," which means that a long, calm stretch of water is followed by a rapid, then another pool. Floating these rivers is easier because they're predictable, and because well-spaced rapids offer time to recover should a canoe be upset. Portaging is easier, too. Rivers with more continuous whitewater present difficulties. Their fast current requires nonstop maneuvering, tiring even the best paddler, as well as leaving little room for error. A river with a sandy bottom usually means slower water—strong current would wash the sand away. Small, shallow rivers can be tricky, unless your canoe is short and maneuverable, while deeper rivers with more volume can have big whitewater, demanding skill, experience, and a well-equipped canoe.

WAVES

When water that is moving fast down a steep gradient meets the slower water of a pool, the fast water piles up on itself, creating stacks of water called *waves*, or occasionally *haystacks*, especially if they're large (six feet or higher). Unlike ocean waves, which move toward shore, river waves are stationary as the current washes through them. Even a one-foot wave looms large for a nervous novice running whitewater the first time. Waves that are clean—without rocks under them, and without tricky back-curling tips—offer a good, fun roller coaster ride. Big waves, however, can swamp a canoe. In an open canoe without added flotation or spray cover, big waves should be avoided, or at least taken off to the side. If you're rigged for whitewater and have identified friendly deep-water waves ahead, go ahead and take them on. Approach a wave head-on and paddle hard to power through it. Sometimes canoeists prefer to quarter through waves, so less water comes onboard.

So-called *rogue waves* may have rocks under them, which may cause a back-curling formation.

This wave can be distinguished by the curl of whitewater forming over the wave's crest. Foil these canoe-swampers by missing them or taking them off to one side.

Veteran canoeists, especially those in decked or covered canoes, enjoy surfing river waves just like on the ocean, except the rider doesn't get washed to shore. To surf a canoe, the paddlers either slow their momentum while entering a wave, or more commonly, eddy out below the

Canoeing through Class II waves. Keep on paddling!

wave and then paddle back upstream into the roller coasters. You should be prepared to swim if you attempt surfing, though—it takes practice to balance against the force of the river.

If you ever find yourself swimming through waves, remember to breathe between waves, in the trough, and hold your breath as you are floated up into the crest—otherwise you'll take in lots of water.

Another set of haystacks.

REVERSALS

When a large volume of water pours over a sharp drop—over a boulder, for instance, or a rock ledge—an interesting phenomenon is created. This river hydraulic is known by many names—*reversal* (because some of the water below the obstacle flows upstream), *hole* or *souse hole* (due to the vertical plunge that creates what appears to be a hole in the river, which the river is constantly trying to fill in), *keeper* or *stopper* (be-

A lowhead dam. Note that the hydraulic extends the full length of the river in an unbroken line—there is no escape from the strong currents. Also note "keeper" action of hydraulic (inset).

cause of the upstream currents that force a canoe or swimmer back into the hole)—or simply as a *hydraulic*.

The reversal is the river at its most powerful, dramatic, and dangerous. As water rushes over the obstacle, a strong undertow is created. The frothy aerated whitewater below such an obstacle offers very little buoyancy. Combined with back-flowing currents, the reversal is a trap for canoes that is best avoided. If you ever do find yourself headed into a reversal, make certain the canoe hits bow first. Paddle hard to propel the canoe through the reversal, digging paddle blades deep to catch the forward-moving water buried below the backward-flowing water on the surface. If you get swept sideways, brace and lean downstream to keep the canoe upright. Experienced white-water canoeists often go "playing" in small hydraulics, after lots of practice in waves and eddies.

Similar hazardous hydraulics form below dams and waterfalls. A special peril for canoeists is the *lowhead dam,* a short dam across the entire width of a river, common around farmlands. These are extremely difficult to detect, as sometimes canyon acoustics produce no telltale sound until it's too late.

To detect the abrupt drop-offs that signal a reversal, dam, or waterfall, look for a horizon line where the river seems to disappear and there is a drop in elevation visible along the distant shorelines. If you spot a horizon line, get to shore immediately and take a look. Other signs of upcoming hydraulics are a very loud roar, spray, or a blind corner. Often, above a big drop-off, a river will pool up, because the obstruction causing the rapid acts on the current like a man-made dam.

Keep a watch for other man-made obstacles. Bridge piers or similar structures should be avoided, as a canoe can be pinned against them by strong current. Along shore, especially, look for rebar—metal bars used to reinforce concrete structures, which can puncture your canoe.

POSITIONING FOR WHITEWATER

Whenever you run rapids, or enter a fast current, always lower your center of gravity so the canoe will be more stable. For many canoeists, the easiest way to do this is to slide down off the canoe seat to their knees. For ultimate balance, have as many contact points with the boat as possible. Serious whitewater paddlers install knee pads, foot braces, and special saddles. When kneeling, spread the knees wide and press them tight against the sides of the canoe. A successful whitewater paddler should strive to be "one with the canoe."

With the proper positioning, even open canoes can run some very powerful rapids. Practice your contact points in easy rapids, and if you aspire to run whitewater often, consider adding some custom braces to your boat.

Leadership in a tandem canoe running rapids depends on positioning as well as experience. Unquestionably, the bow partner gets a better view of what's ahead. The bow not only sits in front but also obstructs the stern's view. The responsibility of sighting obstacles and alerting the stern to their presence is easier for the bow. Yet a route that seems obvious to the bow paddler may not be the best route for the person sitting behind him or her to execute, so communication between partners is important. Partners need to work together and not blame each other for mistakes.

Steering is easier from the stern, except for corrective draw strokes useful for quick rock dodging. Another consideration when deciding who sits where is that the bow is closer to the action, and tends to be a very wet position. Not every canoeist is ready for waves in the face.

WHITEWATER VISION

Being able to see what's coming is crucial for a successful run through whitewater. But a basic feature of rapids is the river dropping abruptly out of sight. Often, you won't be able to see all of a rapid, particularly a difficult rapid, until you're right there, and even while you're running the rapid, surprises can pop up. To counteract this, canoeists scout a rapid before running it. From a safe vantage onshore, paddlers have the luxury of taking a leisurely look at what's coming, planning a route, discussing routes with the partner or other boaters, and watching other boaters run the rapid first.

Because the river drops off sharply, you'll need to visualize how the rapid will look from the canoe, and sight on landmarks that show what spot you were looking at from shore. If there are two mossy rocks in the center of the rapid, for instance, and you've determined that the canoe should go between them, watch for those particular rocks. Some paddlers like to divide the river's width into segments, then visualize their route as dead center, just left of center, far left, along the left shore, and so forth.

Another way to get a better look at what's coming up downstream is to stand up in the canoe. Before you try this in moving water, though, practice first in calm water. Take care to warn your paddling partner first, so he or she can be ready to use a brace for steadying the canoe. Stand up in a slow, even movement, with your legs braced against the seat. Use a sculling motion of the paddle if necessary to maintain your balance while standing. This ability to stand up and look downriver is the canoe's big advantage over kayaks. By sitting higher in the water and being able to stand up, a canoeist enjoys increased visibility.

Backpaddling the canoe slows descent, allowing more time to look over a smaller rapid or find a route through a larger one. If you're still uncertain, land to shore for a quick look. Better to take a second look than to take the wrong route.

BROADSIDE

Never let the canoe drift broadside, or parallel to the current. When broadside, a canoe presents up to five times greater surface area for obstacles like rocks to hit (depending on the length and width of the canoe). When kept straight, the canoe is a much smaller three-foot-wide target. Use the sideslip to maneuver the canoe sideways without turning it broadside.

Should the canoe stray broadside toward a rock or other obstruction (known as broaching), the paddlers should immediately lean *toward* the rock. Your first impulse will be to shy away from the rock, but this will only make things worse. Leaning away from the rock lowers the side opposite the rock, allowing water to pour in, possibly

The brace stroke comes in handy when you're trying to stay upright in rapids.

ROUTE SELECTION THROUGH A "BOULDER GARDEN"

Back ferry or upstream ferry using slow currents of the eddy

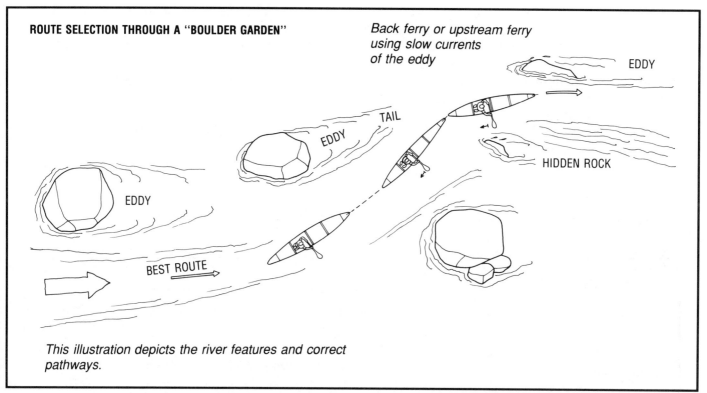

This illustration depicts the river features and correct pathways.

EASY WATER

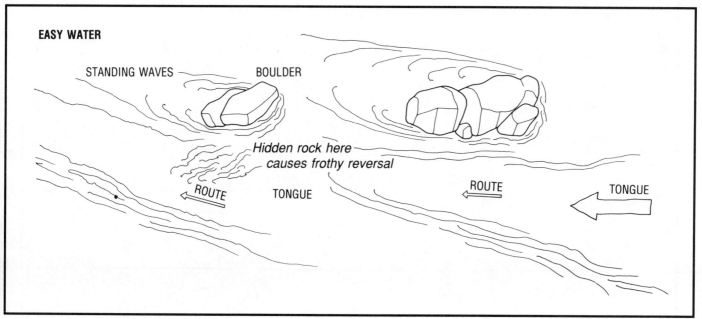

swamping or overturning the canoe. Once filled with water, the canoe can be pinned against the rock by a strong current. By leaning toward the rock, the upstream side of the canoe is raised, presenting the bottom side of the canoe to the current. This allows the current to slide *under* the canoe, often averting an upset or pin situation by rolling the canoe upright.

In a broach situation, make certain you don't get caught "between a rock and a hard place"— between the canoe and the obstruction. A canoe full of water with a modest current pushing it can exert several tons of force against your body. You definitely don't want to wind up squashed between your boat and the rock.

If your canoe wraps around the rock and gets stuck there, getting it loose will be difficult. You'll need rescue equipment such as a Z-drag kit (a system of pulleys and ropes), lots of help, plus a little luck to get the canoe loose.

In a similar situation, a canoe that grounds out on a partially submerged rock in current will be immediately swung sideways by the flow. To recover, brace downstream. Remember, on moving water, always brace downstream, never upstream.

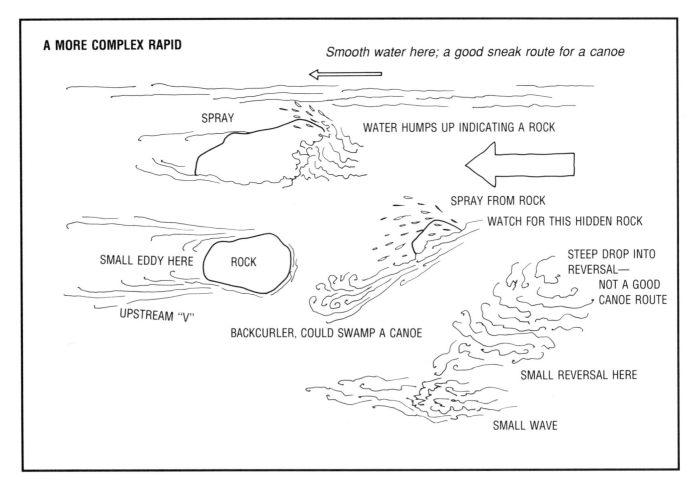

A MORE COMPLEX RAPID

Smooth water here; a good sneak route for a canoe

SPRAY

WATER HUMPS UP INDICATING A ROCK

SPRAY FROM ROCK

WATCH FOR THIS HIDDEN ROCK

SMALL EDDY HERE   ROCK

STEEP DROP INTO REVERSAL—
NOT A GOOD CANOE ROUTE

UPSTREAM "V"

BACKCURLER, COULD SWAMP A CANOE

SMALL REVERSAL HERE

SMALL WAVE

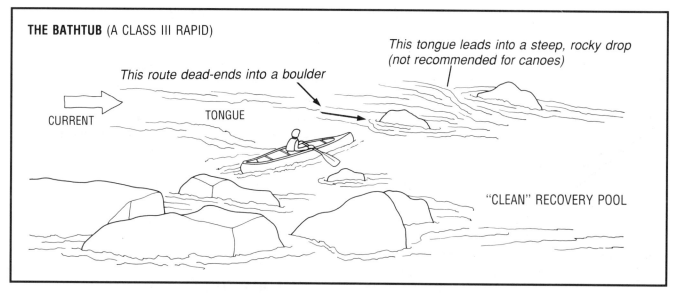

THE BATHTUB (A CLASS III RAPID)

This tongue leads into a steep, rocky drop (not recommended for canoes)

This route dead-ends into a boulder

CURRENT

TONGUE

"CLEAN" RECOVERY POOL

CAN YOU FIND THE CORRECT ROUTE?

FERRYING

Moving back and forth across a current is called *ferrying*, after the method for getting barges across a river by using the current. Canoeists can utilize the river's current to move their craft across the river, too. There are two ways to ferry: the back ferry, in which paddlers face downstream and backpaddle, and the upstream ferry, in which the canoe is pointed upriver and paddled forward. Often, using a ferry angle to cross a river is the best way to avoid upcoming obstacles. With the upstream ferry, point the bow where you want to go, then let the current help shoot you across. With a back ferry, point the bow where you don't want to go.

The secret to making a ferry work is the angle at which the canoe is pointed to take advantage of current. The proper angle—usually about 30 degrees—moves the canoe across river without losing ground downstream, even against a fast current. You must turn the canoe to the proper angle and maintain that angle throughout the ferry maneuver until the canoe is where you want to be. Less angle wastes energy, while more angle is hard to maintain. The precise angle depends on how strong the current is—against a very powerful flow, the angle might have to be 45 degrees.

The upstream ferry is more powerful, but you can't see where the current is taking you. Use the upstream ferry to get across the river quickly, such as at the top of a waterfall you must avoid. Start by turning the canoe upstream at a slight angle—10 degrees—testing the strength of the current. Then gradually angle the canoe into the current. Add more angle if needed. The stern keeps the canoe at the proper angle with draw and pry strokes, constantly adjusting the angle as the current pushes at the canoe. Too much angle stops the ferrying, and means starting over. When ferrying, using a longer paddle in the stern helps to maintain the all-important angle.

The back ferry is useful for dodging obstacles because it slows the canoe down while at the same time moving the canoe across the river. You get a clear view of what's coming by using this maneuver. Back ferrying is simply employing reverse strokes with the canoe at an angle to the current. Usually the 30-degree angle will work in most currents. Besides missing obvious obstacles, the back ferry is useful for ducking slowly around the inside of river bends, avoiding faster currents on the outside that could carry the canoe into trees.

Check your ferrying progress against the shoreline to help maintain perspective of your ferry angle. In strong current, paddle hard to keep the canoe from losing ground. Also remember that the downstream paddler has the best position for correcting the ferry angle.

LANDING THE CANOE

Ferrying assumes more importance as you test your canoeing skills in faster currents, where just landing the canoe to shore becomes more difficult. The elementary yet vital technique of landing a canoe in current often troubles beginners, so practice is in order before you advance to quicker streams. At the top of fast water, plunging over a falls, is no place to be asking, "How do I stop this thing?"

When landing against a current, use the ferry to utilize the power of the river. You'll also need to be able to recognize good landing spots, since a canoe can't stop just anywhere along a river. Current slows near shore, but remember those helical currents that tend to shove a canoe back into the main current. To avoid this, look for eddies.

When landing, always try to go in stern first. Otherwise, the canoe gets swung around by the current. When the stern is put into slower water along shore, the bow will be pulled in. Be sure to choose a landing site that is clear, without other canoes or boats blocking your landing. In a small eddy, the first paddlers to land pull their canoe out of the water, then stand by to help the next boat land, particularly above treacherous rapids.

The upstream-end paddler (generally the stern) gets out first, then steadies the canoe so that the partner can disembark. Don't forget to tie or beach your canoe securely.

THE EDDY TURN

The eddy turn is used to direct the canoe into an eddy. This maneuver can be a real lifesaver, keeping you and your canoe from being swept into big rapids. Eddy turns are a tricky maneuver—you're trying to hit a moving target. To set up for an eddy turn, accelerate paddling speed, aiming as close to the rock as you can. Then the bow paddler executes a draw stroke (or high brace) to grab the eddy water, while the stern (which has not yet crossed the eddy line) does a pry or strong forward sweep stroke on the opposite side. Both paddlers should lean into the turn.

Timing and angle are crucial. When the eddy line is under the canoe, the bow person plants his or her paddle in the eddy with the draw stroke. Try to hit the top of the eddy, where the current is sharpest. Synchronization is important, so when your paddling team practices eddy turns, concentrate on working together.

To exit an eddy try the *peel-out*—an exciting move with flair. First, back up, to make room for the maneuver. The canoe should be pointed up-

BASIC PEEL-OUT

Start with canoe in position, pointed upstream, then angle about 45 degrees.

Bow paddler reaches out to grab current with paddle (draw or brace), canoe swings around. Paddlers should lean into turn.

Proceed downstream

stream at about a 45-degree angle to start across the eddy line. Next, the bow paddler does a hard draw on the river side to catch the outgoing current, as the stern paddles forward. As the bow crosses the eddy line, the bow paddler leans downstream. The stern should support the lean while sweeping the canoe around. When this maneuver is done properly, the canoe whips around impressively into the main current.

Exiting an eddy through the weaker end is also possible, in mild current. However, in turbulent water, the upstream current may be too strong to overcome. Then you'll need the peel-out.

SPECIAL EQUIPMENT FOR WHITEWATER

Canoeist clothing assumes a more important role when you are paddling whitewater. Most fast-moving streams are powered by ice- and snow-melt—very cold water. Also, problems with crossing currents, eddy lines, or impacting obstacles greatly increase opportunities for unexpected swims. The combination of fast and cold water generates a real threat to safety. Follow the "100 Degree" rule: whenever air and water temperature combined equal 100 degrees or less, wear a wet suit or dry suit. For more moderate conditions, paddle jackets and rain gear, with fleece or polypro underneath, are appropriate.

Paddlers in whitewater need helmets for two reasons. First and most obvious are the hard boulders present in most rapids. But also, canoeists always have a hard surface nearby when they dump a canoe—the canoe itself. Special whitewater helmets protect without encumbering. Look for a helmet with secure fasteners that fits you well, plus has openings around the ears so

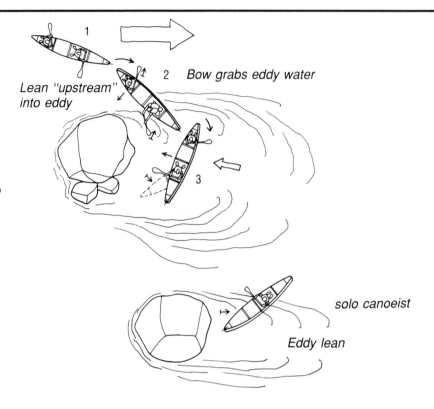

Steps of an eddy turn

1. Approach close to rock-causing eddy

2. Bow does draw or high brace on eddy side to grab eddy water

3. Stern does a forward sweep or pry to aid pulling in

Lean "upstream" into eddy

2 Bow grabs eddy water

3

solo canoeist

Eddy lean

THE PEEL-OUT

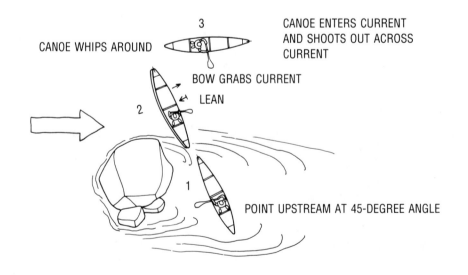

3
CANOE WHIPS AROUND

CANOE ENTERS CURRENT AND SHOOTS OUT ACROSS CURRENT

BOW GRABS CURRENT

LEAN

2

1

POINT UPSTREAM AT 45-DEGREE ANGLE

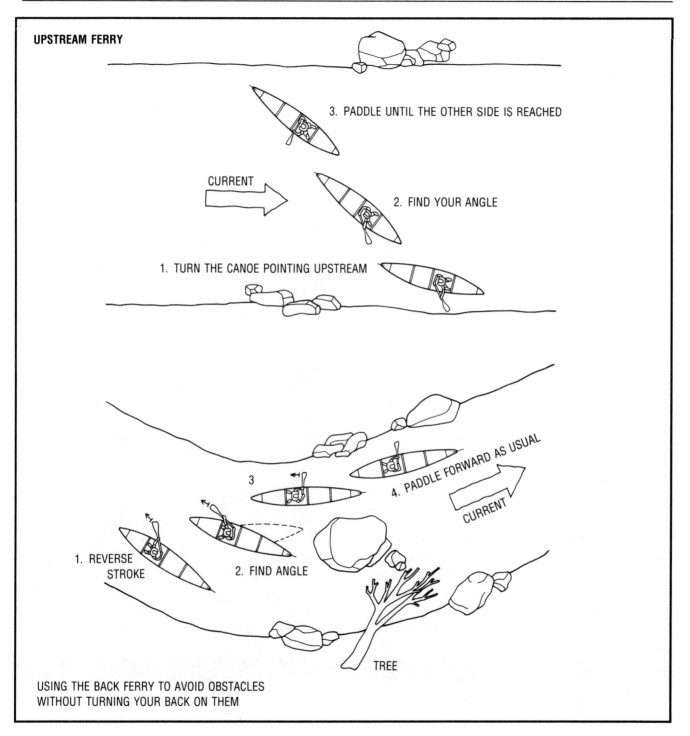

UPSTREAM FERRY

3. PADDLE UNTIL THE OTHER SIDE IS REACHED

CURRENT

2. FIND YOUR ANGLE

1. TURN THE CANOE POINTING UPSTREAM

3

4. PADDLE FORWARD AS USUAL

CURRENT

1. REVERSE STROKE

2. FIND ANGLE

TREE

USING THE BACK FERRY TO AVOID OBSTACLES
WITHOUT TURNING YOUR BACK ON THEM

you can hear warning shouts or the roar of up-coming rapids. (Tie a whistle on your PFD to get the attention of other boaters.)

Whitewater paddlers like to wear an emergency knife on their PFD much like divers use. The knife is used to cut ropes or saw through a spray cover in case of entrapment. Choose a knife that has a quick-release sheath requiring only one hand (your other hand might be trapped) and a blade of stainless steel to foil rust, since the knife will be constantly wet.

Also important is a rescue rope, usually carried in the form of a "throw bag"—sixty to seventy feet of three-eighths-inch soft braided floating polypropylene line, which is stuffed into a nylon bag with a float at the bottom. The loose end of the rope has a loop tied in it, and hangs out of the bag's opening. To use a throw bag, open the drawstring and pull out a short length of line. Hold the loop of this loose end in one hand—securely! With your other hand, throw the bag to the person who needs rescuing. Line feeds out of the bag as it soars over the river. Let the victim know the rope is coming, and to grab the rope (not the bag, as it just keeps feeding out line).

The line is never tied to anyone—rescuer or victim—to avoid entrapment. However, a rescuer can wrap his or her end of the line around a tree or rock, using the current to belay the victim to shore. Belaying is particularly useful for swinging a loose canoe to shore, because it's heavy (especially if full of water). Practice hitting a target with a throw bag before you tackle whitewater. You can throw overhand or underhand—whichever is easiest for you. Restuff the bag carefully, a short length at a time, so the line will feed out properly during the next throw.

Some way of increasing flotation is necessary in whitewater. The canoe must be full of air to float high and resist swamping. This can be achieved with a canoe cover—a custom decked-

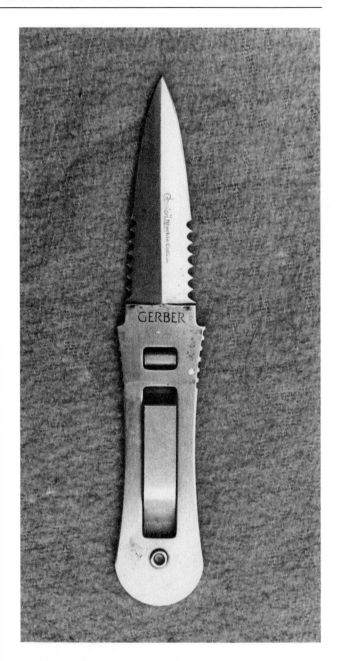

A river knife should be stainless steel and have serrated edges to saw through ropes.

over canoe, or more commonly, a special spray cover that holds in air while excluding water. Or add flotation inside the canoe, in the form of truck tire inner tubes, Styrofoam blocks, or special air bags sold for the purpose. Proper flotation displaces water with air—the trick is keeping the flotation underwater since it wants to float. Tie all flotation in securely, or make sure your spray cover is tightly attached.

Double-check how your PFD is working before attempting any rapids. Is there sufficient flotation to keep your head above water, even in big waves? Be wary of old PFDs that lose flotation as the foam deteriorates from age. If you canoe a lot, you'll need a new life jacket every few years. Also be certain all ties on your PFD are secure. If yours has crotch straps, use them in whitewater.

Keep a spare paddle readily accessible when tackling whitewater. You'll also want all lines secured to avoid entrapment, loops on bow and stern to grab in case of upset, maybe thigh straps to help you stay inside during leans and braces (but beware of entrapment), and perhaps custom-installed knee pads and whitewater saddles for easier kneeling. At the least, you'll want seats that permit kneeling, while not pinning your ankles down.

SPECIAL KNOWLEDGE FOR CANOEING WHITEWATER

In whitewater, knowing self-rescue is vital. After an upset, always stay upstream of the canoe. A fifteen-foot-long canoe in a ten-mile-per-hour current, filled with water, can exert a force of over four tons, easily pinning a hapless swimmer against a rock or bridge pier.

If it's safe, grab an end loop and swim the canoe to shore, or to an eddy, where you can empty out the water and get back in. Or have another canoe perform the canoe-over-canoe rescue. The upright canoeists pull the overturned canoe across the middle of their boat, while the swimmers hold on to the upright canoe. The overturned canoe is then positioned upright, back in the water, and held while the swimmers get back in.

You should know how to swim in rough water before attempting to canoe Class III or greater whitewater. This means floating in a sitting position, with your feet pointed downstream to fend off rocks. Keep your feet off the river bottom to avoid getting a foot caught in an undercut rock, which, when combined with a strong current, could push you underwater. In a moving current, never stand up unless the water is knee-deep or less. If entrapment happens, it's possible to drown in two feet of water. While floating through rapids, use your arms to maneuver. Practice bodysurfing in small waves first, with all your gear on. Also practice rolling your canoe over on flatwater, then climbing back in. You'll have to grab the far gunwale and pull your body flat over the canoe, which takes a little practice.

Stay with your canoe unless it's going where you don't want to go, such as into nasty rapids. In that case, abandon the canoe and head for shore quickly. Go headfirst and try to ferry yourself upstream with the current. If the water is very cold, you must get out as fast as you can, either to shore or into another boat.

Increase your knowledge of whitewater and swift-water safety by joining canoe clubs, taking lessons, or going on outfitted whitewater trips.

THE SHUTTLE

On a river trip, you float from one spot to another. This requires a way to get back to the starting point (unless the current is really slow and you can paddle back upstream). Thus the river shuttle. You can take two or more cars, leaving at least one at each end, then drive back to get the other cars. In popular areas, professional shuttle drivers drive your car to the end of the trip for a fee, or supply a bus to take you back to your car. Or some folks bring along a person who doesn't go down the river, but just drives the shuttle (the "shuttle bunny").

ORGANIZING A TRIP

Organization is important for a river trip. Someone, usually a knowledgeable canoeist called the trip leader, picks a river he or she knows; decides where to put in and take out; chooses rest stops, lunch breaks, and campsites; picks participants according to their skill levels; plans the equipment so everyone has space in a canoe plus the proper gear; files a float plan with a responsible individual (ranger, sheriff); and makes other decisions (what to do if someone is injured, etc.).

Requirements for canoeing whitewater go beyond paddling skills. You must be able to swim and be confident in water, wear a good PFD, possess good equipment, keep your craft under control, maintain the proper distance between canoes (close enough to watch what the next boat is doing without crowding them), watch for hazards and avoid them. Also vital is maintaining good relationships with others along the river, to help keep river access open and rivers running free. Respect rights of anglers and landowners as well as other river users while floating. Keep boat ramps clear for other users. Herd your group together—don't pull out from shore into the middle of another group. You can yell and scream on crowded rivers, but try to blend in while floating through wilderness. Help others in trouble. Don't litter or pollute.

To avoid accidents, watch for the human factor: use of alcohol or drugs, no PFD, unfamiliarity with river, poor skills, poor conditioning, exhaustion, paddling alone. Accidents may also be caused by equipment: not maintained, not intended for rough water, no flotation, no safety gear, no proper clothing. Then there's the environment: high and/or cold water; obstacles like dams, strainers, and undercut rocks; remote areas; bad weather.

Know canoeing emergency signals. For example, most canoeists recognize that a paddle held up horizontally with both hands means stop, pull over, or danger ahead. Three blasts on a whistle means an emergency, as does waving a PFD. A group can develop their own signals, which should include hand signs visible over a distance if shouts can't be heard over crashing waves. And never blow a whistle except to alert another paddler.

CHAPTER 8

CANOE CAMPING

For many people, the best canoe trips happen when the day ends on the water, not in the home driveway. Camping out, whether for a weekend once a year or a four-month cross-country journey through the barrens, adds a special dimension to canoe tripping. If your experiences with camping have been limited to public camps packed with recreational vehicles, the solitude and serenity offered by canoe camping may surprise you. Even just a short paddle up the local reservoir quickly leaves the crowds behind. Many remote areas are accessible only by canoe. Pick your own private island or cove for the night, and enjoy!

Careful planning is important. Decide when and where you want to go, and for how long. Test your skills first on easy day trips, working up to more miles. How many miles a canoe can go in one day depends on the type of canoe, how much load is carried, the paddlers, and the weather conditions. A good average to keep in mind for overnight trips is fifteen miles a day, although good canoeists on flatwater can easily do thirty to fifty miles (without head winds). Remember to start out easy—try a weekender first, then work your way up to longer trips. Get into shape long before a week-long paddle trip. Plan a trip around the skill levels of the group, and work out an itinerary that sets a good pace without tiring anyone.

If you're interested in lengthy expeditions into the wilderness, work on improving your canoe and camping skills until you're ready. The good judgment, self-reliance, and resourcefulness demanded by a real wilderness adventure take time and lots of outdoor experience to develop. Yet the rewards are well worth the effort. Also, start acquiring the quality gear you will need for such a trip, piece by piece if necessary. Preparation is another key to an enjoyable, safe expedition.

Pack overnight gear bags in the middle (amidship) of the tandem canoe. Keep trim in mind while loading.

EQUIPMENT FOR CANOE CAMPING

You can use the same basic equipment for canoe camping as you do for car camping, although you won't be able to take as much. If you have backpacking gear, great. This lightweight equipment will be easy to transport in your canoe, leaving room for a few luxuries. Watch weight, bulk, and suitability for a water environment. Take alumi-

num cooking pots rather than cast iron, unless the trip is short and there are no portages. A sleeping bag that stuffs into a small sack is easier to pack into a dry bag than one that must be rolled into a big lump. Same for sleeping cushions—choose air mattresses or self-inflating pads instead of space-gobbling eggshell foam pads. Many canoeists prefer to avoid down sleeping bags because they are useless once wet, and take a long time to dry out. Even if your bag never receives an accidental dunking, it still could absorb moisture from the damp air around a waterway. Synthetic bags are cheaper than down bags as well.

114

But don't run out and buy a whole new camping outfit tailored for canoeing. Not just yet. For those first few short trips, where you paddle a short distance and stay out only a night or two, preferably on warm summer evenings, you can get by with ordinary gear. As your interest in canoe camping grows and you start to eye a week-long adventure, or even a month's expedition, then add to your collection.

If you've never camped out before, the basic essentials are a sleeping bag and pad/mattress for each person, plus a tent for each group. Small pillows are nice to have, or you can improvise with soft clothing. Practice setting things up in your backyard, or even in the middle of your living room, before you go. (Also make sure your tent's seams get sealed; otherwise they will leak during a rainstorm.) Cut two pieces from a sheet of Visqueen or similar plastic sheeting that match the floor of your tent. Use one underneath the tent floor to protect it from punctures and wear. Use the second groundcloth inside the tent for additional protection.

Tent assignments can be parents in one two-person tent, kids in another, or among groups, people may elect to stay alone in a tent (sharing saves room). With younger children, count on one big tent because the kids will want to sleep close by. With backpack-style tents, choosing a three-person tent for two people offers additional room without compromising on weight and bulk. Whatever tent you choose for canoe camping, make sure the poles are short so they don't stick out of the canoe. Shock-corded poles are much easier to set up than lots of loose pieces. Good tents are reinforced at stress points.

The tent is essential during bad weather or bug attacks, but not absolutely necessary during normal conditions, except for privacy. When you escape the confines of drive-in camping and find your group isolated on a lake island, miles from the nearest neighbors, try sleeping out under the stars for a change. You may never want to go back into your tent.

Early paddlers combined a canvas tarp with their big expedition canoes to form a workable shelter. You can do this too if you're ever caught out in bad weather without a tent, or if one gets damaged, or if you just want to sleep out with some protection from the elements. Carry the canoe up to camp and place it upside down. Prop up one edge with a paddle or stick, then drape a cover (tarp, rain fly, whatever you have) over the open side. In really nasty conditions, or if you don't have anything to use for a cover, you can crawl right under the canoe for protection.

LOADING THE GEAR

Keep trim in mind when loading for a trip. Load gear in the bilge, amidships (except for solo canoes). Avoid overloading—watch your freeboard, the distance from the waterline to the top of the gunwales. Recommended freeboard is a minimum of nine inches. Double-check waterproofing, especially sleeping gear and food. And tie everything down. If thwarts aren't conveniently located for gear tie-downs, glue in D-ring patches on the floor. Some canoeists swear by piling gear loose in the canoe, in case the canoe is lost, but having gear fall out and float away is more likely. Also, a canoe with dry bags strapped in floats higher if upside down and is easier to spot should it escape your control.

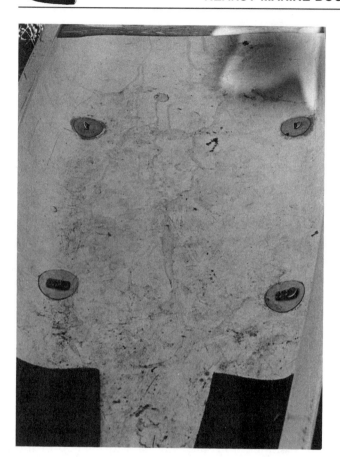

If there are no other handy attachment points for strapping down packs, mount D-rings on the bottom of the canoe.

FOOD SELECTION

Don't diet! Paddling consumes energy, and just being outdoors makes appetites ravenous. Canoeists may need four thousand or more calories per day, so plan on foods that resupply your body with fuel. Besides, paddling also burns fat while building muscle—on a trip of any length, you'll come back leaner, even though you are eating more. Center a long trip around complex carbohydrates—beans and lentils, pasta, rice, wheat flour, freeze-dried potatoes. Then throw in some protein, seasonings, and a few sweets for a balanced and entertaining diet.

On weekenders, meals should be simple. You want to get away from the constant nuisance of cooking. Use fresh foods—fruits, vegetables, meat—and don't worry much about how much things weigh or how they're packed. You can even precook or use special packaging of foods at home so that there are fewer chores to do during your campout. For example, chicken takes about an hour to cook on an outdoor barbecue, but can be zapped in the microwave first to lessen cooking time.

Traditional camp foods are fun to have along, especially for kids, and many are easy to make, even if the wind is blowing hard. Hot dogs broiled on a skewer or grill are both simple and satisfying. Wrap in a slice of bread or bun. Offer an assortment of relish, mustard, onions, or maybe chili to spoon over the 'dogs. A more elaborate camping meal starts at home by cutting up chunks of vegetables and meat for stew or shish kebabs. Sprinkle stew with seasonings, wrap in foil, and pack in a cooler. In camp, just set this foil packet over coals or atop a stove burner. Rotate often so the food doesn't burn. Each camper can do his or her own, so they cook faster than one big package.

Kebabs grill fast over coals or charcoal. Skewer chunks of onion, pineapple, cherry tomatoes, whole mushrooms, green pepper, and tender meat (beef, pork, or lamb works, as does precooked poultry—or tofu for the vegetarian). Take along a sweet-and-sour or barbecue sauce and slather over the kebabs a few minutes before they're done (don't add a sugary sauce too early, or it will burn). Most all barbecue foods work well for canoe camping, although on a cool evening you may prefer a bowl of soup or a casserole like macaroni and cheese.

For a quickie dessert, try S'mores, the camping classic. Toast marshmallows on skewers until done (depends on individual preference). Meanwhile, split a graham cracker in two and divide a Hershey chocolate bar in half. Layer graham cracker, marshmallow, chocolate half, marshmallow, graham cracker—or use only one marshmallow. Also try peanut butter spread on the crackers. The name S'mores came from the request "Can I have some more?"

Another tasty main course, quick to cook, is stir-fry. Cut vegetables into thin slices at home (or buy a packet of precut veggies at the supermarket). Most people enjoy carrots, broccoli, cauliflower, Chinese bok choy, celery, water chestnut, pea pods, zucchini, green pepper, onion, and mung bean sprouts. (Use Chinese vegetables fresh if you wish—a can is more convenient.) In the camp kitchen, sort vegetables according to how long each takes to quick fry. Use a sturdy fry pan or wok. Pour in a little cooking oil, then toss in the tougher vegetables first. Cook over high temperature with constant stirring, adding the rest of the vegetables. Use nuts (particularly cashews) to add crunch. Fresh meat can be cooked right along with the veggies, or try a can of chunk turkey. Top with a packet of stir-fry seasoning mixed with soy sauce. Serve with rice or noodles (these could be the precooked kind that only need to be warmed up—do this right in the wok to avoid dirtying a second pan).

REFRIGERATION

On trips of less than a week, carrying an ice chest is feasible. Consider a "soft" chest that collapses flat after the food and ice are gone. Freeze jugs of water for ice—then you can have ice water when it melts.

Be meticulous in avoiding food spoilage. You don't want to get sick on your canoe campout. Meats, especially, should be kept directly on ice and used within a day or two. Seal in plastic bags to contain juices that may contaminate other foods. Use a cooler tray for fragile items like eggs and strawberries, and to keep foods out of meltwater.

After the ice is gone, some foods can be kept chilled by placing them directly on the bottom of the canoe, where cold water provides the refrigeration. Things like cheese and vegetables keep well in this manner, but don't try meats.

FOOD FOR LONGER TRIPS

For trips approaching a week or more, try to cut down on food packaging. Empty packaged foods into plastic bags, then write the cooking instructions on the bag, or tear the instructions off the package and seal with the food. Premeasure ingredients as much as possible, using powdered milk and eggs that can be reconstituted with water at the campsite.

Longer trips require careful meal planning and shopping. You'll need to have dehydrated and freeze-dried foods. Things like supermarket macaroni and cheese are possible, but you can't beat a meal that's prepared simply by adding boiling water and waiting five minutes.

Many expedition planners dry their own foods to save money, and to have better-tasting foods. Most fruits and vegetables can be dried at home, in the oven, or better, in a home food dryer. Canned goods like tomato sauce can be poured out and dried like fruit leather, then used in camp to create spaghetti sauce or chili. Jerky makes a satisfying snack or quick meal.

Look for exotic foods when expedition shopping. For example, Oriental shops offer dried shiitake mushrooms, dried shrimp, and other specialties to enliven a camp menu. Pack along plenty of spices and seasonings for creative cooking.

Most foods should be dry, but a few cans are acceptable, especially if you are mailing food packages ahead, or buying in remote areas. Select canned fish (especially tuna) for high protein, corned beef hash, Spam, pineapple or other fruits (great for desert trips, as they provide juices, too). Poor choices are canned drinks (powdered mixes go further) or milk (same reason). Write contents of can in Magic Marker in case the label gets soaked off.

For fresh wilderness food, sprouting can't be beat. Pack along alfalfa, mung beans, lentils, or other good sprouting seeds to enjoy. Soak seeds overnight in clean water (not lake or river water), then drain and place in sprouting container (a plastic bottle with a mesh-lined lid works). Flush with clean water several times a day. Your sprouts will be ready to enjoy in a few days, depending on the air temperature. Use them in sandwiches, stir fry, salads, or sprinkled on top of hot soup.

CAMP STOVES

Most cooking should be done over a camp stove. These are faster, more convenient, and better for the environment than cooking fires. Also, the bottoms of your cooking pots won't turn black from soot. Most canoeists choose either a white gas stove (which is cheaper, with refillable containers, and burns hotter, but must be primed or pumped before cooking) or a propane stove (disposing of cylinders can be a problem, but on short trips, you can use a combination cooker/heater propane unit).

Don't forget to pack matches in a waterproof container. If the matches are safety matches, the entire matchbox must be kept dry for a striking surface. Kitchen matches can strike on any dry surface. Unfortunately, all waterproof matches are safety matches. The best way to avoid striking surface hassles is to use regular kitchen matches waterproofed at home. A good method is putting an entire box in a vacuum-sealed plastic bag. Or dip each match in paraffin. Packing along extra matches, butane lighters, and special stove igniters is a good idea, particularly on an expedition.

Don't forget the cookset, eating utensils, and a sharp knife. A fillet knife with a stainless steel blade (won't rust) in a plastic sheath (won't harbor germs) works exceptionally well as an all-purpose kitchen knife. The tip is protected, and many models selling for ten dollars or less have built-in sharpeners. Because the plastic sheath is easy to clean and sterilize (with household bleach), a fillet knife is more sanitary to use than an ordinary sheath knife in leather. Folding knives are almost impossible to keep clean. Don't wear your knife unless it's a whitewater safety knife (which does double duty as a kitchen knife if you remember to clean it completely); otherwise it just gets in the way of paddling.

OTHER GEAR

You'll soon develop a comprehensive checklist for packing overnight trips. Some things you don't want to forget are a small flashlight with extra batteries (useful for finding your sleeping space after dark, or reading in bed). For sanitation as well as convenience, each person should have a personal drinking cup, eating utensils, and water bottle. For personal hygiene, take biodegradable soap, toilet paper (remove the inside cardboard to make more compact), grooming items (shaver, toothbrush and paste, etc.), plus a small towel. The group should have a first aid kit with bandages and medications.

Also carry sun protection (waterproof sunscreen, Chap Stick, brimmed hat), skin lotion (especially for desert trips or windy trips), bug repellent, map and compass (important for off-water hiking, as well as route finding along waterways with numerous side channels). Luxury items include camera gear and film in a waterproof container, camp shoes (hiking boots are good for portaging), a foot pump for air mattresses, a Thermos for carrying coffee (or hot water and drink/soup mixes, wonderful in cold weather), and a mesh bag for chilling drinks in the river.

Always handy in camp are garbage bags and extra self-sealing plastic bags, shovel or trowel (for latrine digging), compact table (the Roll-a-Table takes up little room), cooking grill (for barbecues), bucket for washing dishes and self, Solar Shower (nice on long trips if you have hot weather to heat the water), and camp chairs (float cushions or canoe chairs do double duty).

SAFE WATER SUPPLY

Even in wilderness, water can be unsafe. Beaver, cattle, and other animals carry and spread *Giardia* parasites. To guarantee safe water, you can carry tap water in jugs, refill at springs, and purify the rest. Filters or chlorine/iodine tablets provide the safest purification. Be sure a filter works for *Giardia* before using. Stretch your water supply with a few canned beverages if weight is not critical. Also, you can boil suspect water, but boil hard at least ten minutes.

ANIMALS IN CAMP

Fortunately, sealing food in watertight containers also reduces odors that attract animals like bears. Even so, it's best to be prepared at night. Store food in waterproof bags, and leave them sealed until use. Hang food bags from trees in bear country, and don't leave tempting ice chests sitting in canoes (bears have been known to destroy a boat trying to get food). Also, don't have any food items around your tent or sleeping areas, and don't go to bed without washing up. Keep food and sleeping areas separate. In bear country, check with rangers about what areas to avoid. Plan meals carefully to avoid leftovers—burn any scraps (in small bits) in the fire, along with empty cans (pack these out after burning). Most animals are interested only in a free meal, not in bothering you. Loud noises chase away intruders; try banging pots together or blasting your whistle. And never feed wild animals or leave food or garbage behind—even buried.

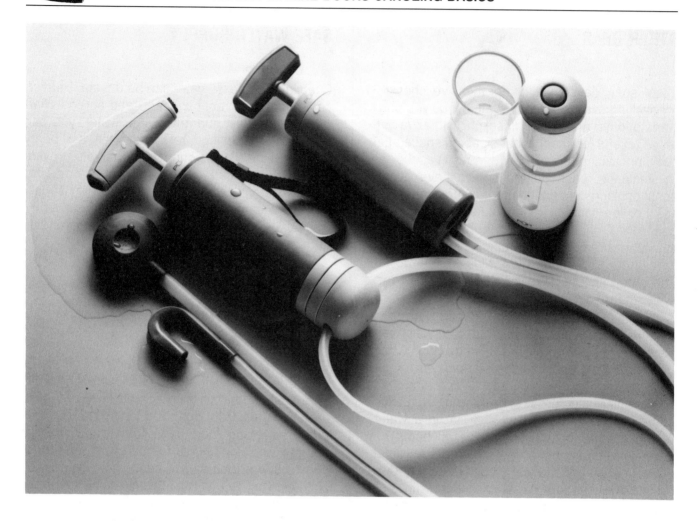

Water filters eliminate worries about unsafe drinking water, transforming any stream or lake into pure, good-tasting water almost instantly.

LOW-IMPACT CAMPING

To reduce the impact of your visit to the wilds, try to utilize existing sites, rather than stomping down new tent areas. Choose sandy beaches or gravel bars for campsites when appropriate because these sites are washed clean by the waterway.

Don't build a fire unless you can keep it small and contained. Many regions restrict fires; you may need a firepan (a metal box that holds the fire) to be legal. Don't drag a big log into camp to burn in the fire, or break limbs off trees. Choose driftwood chunks no thicker than your wrist whenever possible. Driftwood makes a hot fire that burns down to clean ash, and is replenished every season. Use a camp stove for most or all cooking. Avoid cutting vegetation—bring skewers, tent poles, etc., with you and take them out when you leave.

Trenching tents isn't done anymore. Use a plastic sheet cut to just smaller than the tent's bottom to allow drainage. On unlevel ground, position tents so heads are uphill and the door is downhill—don't smooth out ground.

Remember the biodegradable soap. Wash both bodies and dishes well away from the water's edge, using a bucket, bailer, or cook pot. For human waste, use existing facilities whenever available. In forested environments, urinate away from camp into the trees; along desert waterways, urinate directly into the river (urine won't biodegrade very fast in sterile desert soils, and the heat makes it smell, while the river whisks it away—this won't pollute a major waterway). For solid waste, select a site far from any water source, campsite, or beach (sand doesn't allow biode-grading). Then dig a small hole about six inches deep. Set out a clump of topsoil that you replace in the hole after use. Burn or pack out toilet paper rather than leaving it behind (same for feminine hygiene products). Nowadays, some waterways require groups to carry Porta Pottis or other human waste containment systems. Use them only to pack out solid waste or the containment system will be overwhelmed. Set up a garbage bag for toilet paper and a bucket for urine that is later dumped into an appropriate site.

Lastly, police your site for litter before you leave. Worst offenders are spent propane cylinders, plastic twist-ties from bread wrappers, cigarette butts, and aluminum cans. If you come across garbage left by thoughtless campers, pack it out with you. Remember, never bury garbage.

APPENDIX

THE INTERNATIONAL SCALE OF WHITEWATER DIFFICULTY

With this system, employed worldwide, whitewater is rated on a scale of Class I through Class VI, with Class I being easy water and Class VI virtually unrunnable.

Remember that this scale is only a guide and is often interpreted differently by different paddlers. Consult several sources. Know that rapids change, as well, especially during periods of high water. A moderate river could easily be transformed into a Class V nightmare should the river rise suddenly. Strainers can appear overnight. Other factors that increase the degree of difficulty should be taken into consideration, too, when investigating a run, such as remoteness, water temperature, distance between rapids, and difficulty of rescue.

Class I—*Very Easy*. Moving water with a few riffles and small waves. Few or no obstructions.

Class II—*Easy*. Rapids with waves up to three feet and wide, clear channels obvious without scouting. Some maneuvering required.

Class III—*Medium*. Rapids with high, irregular waves often capable of swamping an open canoe. Rapids with narrow passages that may require complex maneuvering. Scouting from shore may be necessary.

Class IV—*Difficult*. Long rapids; waves powerful and irregular. Dangerous rocks and boiling eddies. Passages difficult to scout; powerful and precise maneuvering required in very turbulent waters, constricted passages. Scouting from shore often necessary, and rescue may be difficult. Generally not possible for open canoes. Boaters in covered canoes should be able to Eskimo roll.

Class V—*Very Difficult.* Extremely difficult, long, and very violent rapids, following each other almost without interruption; highly congested routes. Scouting mandatory but often difficult. Risk of boat damage and serious injury to paddlers. For teams of experts with excellent equipment. Ability to Eskimo roll is essential for paddlers in covered canoes.

Class VI—*Extraordinarily Difficult.* Difficulties of Class V carried to extremes of navigability. Nearly impossible and very dangerous. For team of experts only, at favorable water levels and after close study with all precautions.

CANOEING VOCABULARY

Amidships—the middle or center of a canoe

Bailer—a container used to scoop water out of a canoe

Beam—width; the widest part of a canoe

Bilge—curvature between bottom and side of a canoe, often used to refer to the inside middle of a canoe where gear is carried

Board—to climb onto or into a boat

Bow—the front end of a canoe

Broach—to turn sideways suddenly, in wind or on a river; to contact a rock or other obstacle while sideways

Broadside—turned crossways to the current, exposing the broad side to obstacles

Carry—to pick up and walk with a canoe; see *Portage*

Carrying capacity—the amount of weight a canoe can safely float

Class—short for classification; the degree of difficulty presented by a river rapid, according to the International Scale of Whitewater Difficulty

Deck—a solid covering put over the top of a canoe to ward off whitewater; or, panels attached to bow and stern that act like a miniature deck

Decked canoe—a canoe with a hard covering over the top, designed for whitewater use

Depth—the measurement of a canoe from top of gunwales to bottom

Draft—the amount of water it takes to float a canoe

Eddy—quiet water that forms behind a river obstacle such as a rock

Entrapment—having part of the body caught up in loose rope, undercut rocks, or part of the canoe, such as too-low seats; life-threatening if the body is forced underwater by the entrapment

Flatwater—lake or slow-moving river with no whitewater

Flotation—buoyant material, either built-in or placed inside, as float bags, to make the canoe float even if swamped or overturned

Footbrace—a bar or bundle that a paddler uses to brace the feet during paddling

Freeboard—the measurement from the waterline of a canoe to the top of the gunwales amidships, used to determine if a canoe is overloaded (nine inches of freeboard is a safe minimum)

Gunwales (pronounced, and sometimes spelled, *gunnels*)—the railing around the outer rim of a canoe

Helical currents—spiral currents that develop along the shore of a river, which tend to push a swimmer or boat back into the main current

Horizon line—a line across a river at the top of a drop-off, where the river appears to disappear, and shoreline elevation drops off abruptly; often signals a rapid dangerous to canoes

Hull—the basic shell of a canoe

Initial stability—a canoe's resistance to tipping when stepping in or out; best in flat-bottomed canoes. See *Secondary stability*

Keel—a line on the canoe's bottom, down the middle, from bow to stern. Originally, a strip of wood or aluminum attached to a canoe's bottom, thought to make the canoe track better and stay on course when the wind blows. Now *keel* often refers to keel line, or an invisible line where the keel would be.

Keel line (or *centerline*)—the line down the middle of the canoe, whether visible or imaginary. Important for balancing. When stepping into a canoe, center your weight over this line for proper balance. Also, the line of travel when tracking straight.

Kevlar—brand name for space-age fiberglass hull material, also used in bulletproof vests

Leeward—sheltered place out of the wind

Line—rope used in canoeing

Livery—canoe rental shop

Lowhead dam—a concrete structure usually built across the entire length of a river, allowing water flow over the top which creates dangerous hydraulics at the bottom of the drop

Nose—the end, or tip, of a canoe, usually the bow tip

Painter—a line attached to the bow or stern of a canoe, used to tie up, pull around obstacles, or as a safety hold; also useful for tying the canoe down to the bumper of a car

PFD—Personal Flotation Device. Life jacket, vest, or throw cushion. Look for Coast Guard approval.

Pivot—to turn sharply

Playboat—a craft designed for high maneuverability, suitable for "playing" (surfing waves, riding holes, etc.) in whitewater

Portage—to carry a canoe over land

Reversal—a river feature created by fast current dropping over a rock or ledge, also called *hole* or *souse hole, keeper* or *stopper, hydraulic;* dangerous to canoes

Ribs—like human ribs, curved supports that supply hull rigidity and structural strength

Rocker—the amount of upward curve of a canoe's keel line. Rocker varies from one to five inches, with two inches being average. The more rocker, the quicker a canoe will pivot. Extreme rocker is for serious whitewater boats, while mild rocker is for flatwater boats.

Royalex—brand name for heavy-duty plastic hull material

Scout—to walk along shore and look over a rapid or stretch of river prior to paddling

Seaworthiness—a canoe's ability to handle rough water

Secondary stability—also called *final stability.* A canoe's resistance to tipping in heavy water. Best in round hull. Note that canoes that initially feel stable when you step into them are easily tipped over in big waves.

Shuttle—transportation back to the starting point of a river trip. A shuttle can mean having your car driven around by a paid driver, riding back in another vehicle to the starting point, or even carrying a bicycle along to get back to your car.

Skid plate—a layer of extra material applied to the underside of the bow to aid in abrasion resistance, especially when the canoe is beached

Solo canoe—canoe designed for one paddler sitting amidships.

Splash cover—a fabric cover that fits over the top of a canoe, like a deck, to keep out water; used in whitewater, also useful for keeping paddlers' lower bodies out of wind and rain

Swamp—to fill with water

Swamped—full of water, as from a wave

Tandem—a canoe built for two paddlers sitting in bow and stern

Throw bag—a bag stuffed with rope used in river rescues

Thwart—a cross brace on a canoe, between port and starboard gunwales; not meant to be used as a seat—for structural integrity only

Track—to move in a straight line; to line or rope the canoe upstream against the current

Trim—a canoe's balance while floating; a properly trimmed canoe sits level in the water

Tumblehome—an inward curving of a canoe's sides above the waterline, shaped like the letter *C* on its left side

Waterline—a horizontal line where the water's surface encounters the sides of a canoe

Whitewater—rapids on a river. The name derives from turbulence generating frothy, air-filled water that appears white.

Yoke—a special frame designed to carry a canoe over long portages

LIST OF CANOE AND EQUIPMENT RESOURCES

Canoe Rentals

**National Association of
Canoe Liveries and Outfitters**
Box 248
Butler, KY 41006
(606) 472-2205

Source for addresses of canoe rentals and canoe guides

Canoe Manufacturers

Alumacraft Boat Co.
315 St. Julien
St. Peter, MN 56082
(507) 931-1050
Aluminum canoes

Grumman
4170 Veterans Memorial Hwy.
Bohemia, NY 11716
(516) 737-5400
Aluminum canoes

Old Town Canoe Co.
58 Middle St.
Old Town, ME 04468
(207) 827-5514
Plastic, wood, fiberglass, fiberglass-Kevlar canoes

We-no-nah Canoes
P.O. Box 247
Winona, MN 55987
(507) 454-5430
Fiberglass and Kevlar canoes

Dagger Canoe
P.O. Box 1500
Harriman, TN 37748
(615) 882-0404

Mad River Canoe
P.O. Box 610
Waitsfield, VT 05673
(802) 496-3127

Coleman
P.O. Box 1762
Wichita, KS 67201
(316) 261-3211
Ram-X polyethylene canoes

Mohawk Canoes
963 N. Hwy. 427
Longwood, FL 32750
(407) 834-3233
Fiberglass, Kevlar, Royalex; also paddles, whitewater customizing kits

Lincoln Paddle-Lite Canoes
RR2 Box 106
Freeport, ME 04032
(207) 865-0455
Lightweight fiberglass and Kevlar canoes

American Traders
627 Barton Rd.
Greenfield, MA 01301
(413) 773-9631
"World's largest selection of wooden canoes"

Western Canoeing Inc.
P.O. Box 115
1717 Salton Rd.
Abbotsford, B.C.
Canada V2S 4N8
(604) 853-9320

Paddles

Werner Paddles
12322 Hwy. 99 S. #100
Everett, WA 98204
(800) 275-3311

Sawyer Paddles & Oars
P.O. Box 624
Rogue River, OR 97537
(503) 535-3606

Carlisle Paddles
P.O. Box 488
Grayling, MI 49738
(517) 348-9886

Canoe Outfitters

Madawaska Kanu Camp
Box 635
Barry's Bay, Ont.
Canada K0J 1B0
(613) 756-3620
Summer address for whitewater canoe/kayak camp

Great Canadian Ecoventures
P.O. Box #25181
Winnipeg, Man.
Canada R2V 4C8
Trips in remote areas, beginners welcome

Miscellaneous

Voyageur
P.O. Box 207
Mad River Green
Waitsfield, VT 05673
(802) 496-3127
Canoe accessories: seats, PFDs, roof racks, flotation

Wyoming River Raiders
601 S.E. Wyoming Blvd.
Casper, WY 82609
(808) 247-6068
Canoe gadgets, carts, roof racks, river sandals, rescue ropes, etc.

Nantahala Outdoor Center
41 Hwy. 19 W.
Bryson City, NC 28713
(800) 367-3521
Guided trips, instruction, canoes, gear

Northwest River Supplies
209 S. Main
Moscow, ID 83843
(208) 882-2383
Source for general whitewater gear

Primex of California
P.O. Box 505
Benicia, CA 94510
(707) 746-6855
Straps, repair materials, canoe carts, helmets, gloves, etc.

General Canoeing Information

American Canoe Association
8580 Cinderbed Rd.
P.O. Box 1190
Newington, VA 22122

Canadian Recreational Canoeing Association
1029 Hyde Park Rd., Suite 5
Hyde Park, Ont.
Canada N0M 1Z0
(519) 473-2109

Canoe Carts

Farrington Chariots
Box 6293
Santa Rosa, CA 95406
(707) 576-8010

Canadian Boat Walker
Classic Canoes
627 Barton Rd.
Greenfield, MA 01301
(413) 773-9631

Inflatable Canoes

SOAR Inflatables
507 N. 13th St. #409
St. Louis, MO 63103
(314) 436-0016

B & A Distributing Co.
201 S.E. Oak St.
Portland, OR 97214
(503) 230-0482
Wholesale importer of inflatables, information about Eurocraft inflatable canoes

Hybrids

Wayak
P.O. Box 392
Lincoln, CA 95648
(916) 989-9771

Saroca Products
Box 468
159 Route 3A
Sagamore Beach, MA 02562
(508) 888-1220

Pak Boats
P.O. Box 700-T
Enfield, NH 03748
(603) 632-7654
folding canoes

INDEX